P9-CJX-477

SHOT HAPPENS

I got shot
What's your problem?

Mike Schlappi

Mike Schlappi Communications
© 2009 by Mike Schlappi Communications
All rights reserved. Published 2009

ISBN 978-1-61584-247-6

First paperback edition revised and expanded 2001:
    Bulletproof Principles for Striking Gold
Second paperback edition revised 2003 with new title:
    Bulletproof Principles for Personal Success
Third edition revised 2009 with new title:
    Shot Happens: I Got Shot. What's Your Problem?

Cover designer: Jack White
Creative Editor: Tom Cantrell
Editing/Proofread team: Rich Hopkins, Tami Schlappi, Cherie Brunatti,
Megan Schlappi, Kathie Leany, Joseph Gibbons and Karen Hall
Aviation experts: Brian Golding, Art Bobrowitz and Frank Coprivnicar

Published by Mike Schlappi Communications
Printed and bound in the United States of America
by Transcript Bulletin Publishing

This book may not be reproduced in whole or in part, by electronic or
any other means which exist or may yet be developed, without written
permission of the author—except for brief quotations used in reviews or
presentations—in which credit must be given to the author.

Contents

Prologue

"I got shot. What's your problem?"

Does that sound sardonic or terse or dismissive? I don't mean it that way. I *did* get shot—and it *is* my problem. A .38 caliber bullet fired at point-blank range, slammed into my chest, clipped my lung, narrowly missed my heart, and lodged in my spine, paralyzing me from the chest down—and I had to deal with it. I still have to deal with it every day. That is my problem.

Now, what's *your* problem? What do *you* have to deal with today—or every day? Do you have something lodged in you—maybe not in your spine, but perhaps in your heart or mind—that causes you pain and makes you feel paralyzed one way or another?

What position are you taking relative to your problem? In other words, what is your *attitude* relative to your situation? Technically that is what attitude is: simply a position.

I blush to use the old, tired, technique of starting a book or speech with a dictionary definition of the subject. However, since the primary objective of this book is to clarify the meaning of the word *attitude*, and use our enhanced understanding of the word to enhance our response to life, I guess it is reasonable to at least mention its definition.

Every dictionary I have consulted (including a bible dictionary) agrees that attitude is a position. Be it physical or mental, emotional or spiritual, social or financial, attitude is the position that one takes relative to one's situation, circumstance, or environment. You see, in my book (and this is my book ☺), attitude is a *position* not a *mood*; it is the position we take toward our circumstances that turns bad days into good days. Why do I believe that? Why do I *know* that? What makes me the *attitude authority*? Well, here's my story.

CHAPTER 1

This Isn't Real

Icould already hear the roar of the crowd and the delighted shrieks of the cheerleaders—especially that cute brunette with the amazing smile—as I crashed through the screen door, slamming it back against the side of the house. I was the quarterback, and buddy, we were going to win this one!

I cleared the three front steps in one long jump then quickly cut right, faking out the neighbor's terrier as if avoiding a tackle in the approaching championship game.

My soft rubber football cleats dug into the freshly-cut lawn as I raced through two neighbors' yards, leaped a hedge, then cut across the road to my teammate's house to pick him up for our final practice before the big game.

Today was going to be a great day. I knew it. I could feel it. I had never felt more alive. I had looked forward to this game for months. Our team had survived the All-Star football playoffs and we were to play our arch rivals from Provo for the championship.

It was Veteran's Day, five weeks shy of my fifteenth birthday. I was young, filled with energy, and in perfect shape. I had been blessed with unusual coordination and athletic skill. I was quick and agile and I loved physical competition.

Because I was the quarterback, I was responsible for leading my team to victory. I was serious about my role. I always tried hard not to act like I was more important than anyone else on the team, but inside I did feel special and very lucky. I knew I had great promise and potential and dreamed of being an accomplished athlete, maybe even a pro.

Like Superman, I leaped the steps to my friend Torrey's front porch in a single bound, and banged on his door. I ran in place, feeling ten feet tall. My adrenaline was pumping and I could hardly wait to get to the football field. I had never been accused of being patient, especially when a big game was only a day away.

"Come on in!" Torrey yelled from the back of the house. I headed in the direction of his voice. He was still getting dressed, so I just wandered around the house, pausing a moment to watch a couple of minutes of the popular sitcom, "All in the Family." The grass clippings on my cleats left traces of the neighbors' lawns wherever I walked. I was oblivious to the mess I was making.

Torrey was in the bathroom that adjoined his parent's bedroom. I plopped down on the edge of their bed and looked around. I noticed his father's .38 caliber revolver on the nightstand. Torrey's dad was a police officer. This was his off-duty pistol.

Boys are fascinated with guns. I had grown up in a household where hunting was an important family tradition, so I was naturally curious. I leaned over and picked up the pistol. It was in a brown leather case, worn shiny with age, and the flap was snapped closed.

Torrey bounded into the room and grabbed the holstered gun from me.

"Mike, look!" He slid the pistol from its case, casually flipped open the cylinder, and shook out the bullets. I watched as four shiny stainless steel bullets fell to the bed. One, two, three, four—I counted them as they bounced onto the white bedspread. They looked cool, all silver and sleek.

Torrey snapped the cylinder closed and spun it. I wondered nervously how many bullets this gun held but there was no time. He pointed the gun at my chest—and pulled the trigger.

That instant—that agonizing, life-altering split second–became the most often replayed moment of my life—and Torrey's too, I'm sure.

There was an earsplitting explosion, a flash of light and a blast of blue smoke as the gun went off. A .38 caliber slug burned a neat hole through my shirt, ripped into my chest, clipped my lung and slammed into my spine, knocking me violently backwards onto the bed.

The bullet had brushed past my heart, and lodged between two vertebrae. I instantly lost all feeling from my chest down. The slug didn't sever the spinal cord; it was the shock that paralyzed me. My body convulsed and shook while my mind struggled to comprehend.

This can't be happening. This isn't real.

But it was. It was one of those moments where the course of your life changes immediately and irrevocably—and though you want to deny it—you know it's real.

It would be months, even years, before either of us would feel the full impact of that bullet. Fortunately for me, the outcome of this paralyzing moment would ultimately become positive, setting me on a path of great opportunity and even greater blessings.

Throwing the gun down as if it had turned red-hot in his hands, Torrey ran from the room crying out unintelligibly in shock and disbelief. I could hear him running through the house, weeping, mumbling, pounding on the piano keys and throwing things around in a frantic effort to somehow rearrange this horrifying reality. I tried to call out to him to get him to phone my mother, but for some reason it was hard for me to speak—and Torrey was too busy freaking out to do anything as sensible as call for help.

I called out weakly, trying to calm him down. For some reason, I felt more concern for him than myself, but I also desperately needed his help. Getting help from him in his condition apparently wasn't an option, however, so I had to make the call. I reached for the cord dangling from a turquoise blue princess phone on the wall above the bedside table, but I couldn't reach it. My body, now paralyzed from the chest down, kept me pinned to the bed like a huge leaden anchor.

The bullet had drilled through a corner of my right lung, and my lung and chest cavity were filling with blood, making breathing progressively difficult.

I needed to move—but nothing would respond to my mental commands. Two-thirds of what, just a moment ago, was a perfect, young athlete's body, was now nothing but dead weight. No response, no balance. I was stuck.

My whole body felt heavy, as if glued to the bed, waiting for my next command, yet unable to respond. I was conscious and keenly aware, but in shock. I was beginning to panic. I could still hear Torrey yelling and throwing dishes in the kitchen. If I was going to survive, I had to calm him down so he could call for help, and I had to do it quickly, or I was a goner.

I tilted my head and looked down along my body to see where my legs were. Reaching down with my right hand, I grasped my thigh. I was surprised that there was absolutely no feeling—not like it was a little numb but like it was someone else's leg—it was completely dead. I could feel my leg with my hand, but my leg could not feel my hand. Weird.

Time slowed. The pain increased even as my comprehension decreased. It seemed an eternity before Torrey reentered the room. He leaned over me with panic in his eyes, grabbed my shoulders and shook me as if I was playing a joke on him. "C'mon Mike, get up—what's the matter—don't do this. Quit kidding around!" Torrey paused, anxiously searching my face, hoping I would grin and jump up. "Quit it!" He screamed, "You're faking it! Get up! You're faking it!"

What's happening? In the gathering fog, questions rose in slow motion in my confused mind. *Why is he screaming? Why can't I breathe?*

I had to get Torrey to calm down. I pulled my shirt up so he could see that he had really shot me. The wound was small, but it was shocking to see a hole in my chest and a crimson trickle running down my side and staining the white bedspread. *Where is my heart? Am I dying? Is that why I can't breathe? Why can't I move?*

When Torrey finally accepted the reality that I was not faking and was, in fact, terribly wounded, he grabbed the blue handset off the wall and dialed my home number.

He was shaken—his whole body was shaking. "Mrs. Schlappi come quick, Mike's been hurt!" he screamed into the phone. I wondered if his vocal cords would snap.

"Calm down, Torrey. It's okay," I whispered. I tried to get him to give Mom the address but he could only blurt out a panic-stricken, "Just hurry!" He abruptly hung up the phone and ran from the room again.

Fortunately, we lived only a few houses away. Mom must have recognized Torrey's voice, because she was there in an instant.

I was still conscious when she came into the room. She had those big '70s giant rollers in her hair that gave her the look of a worried Martian.

"Gee, Mom, you look nice today," I said faintly, grinning up at her from the bloodstained bed. Then I blacked out. Somewhere in the midst of this nightmare of increasing bewilderment and pain, I realized that I wasn't just hurt, I was mortally wounded and, barring a miracle, I was going to die.

I had known this was going to be a special day, but being shot by a .38 police special is not the kind of "special" I had in mind. I started out the day feeling *really alive* and I did not want to end it by being *really dead*.

I asked God to please let me live. I promised Him that if He would let me live, I would be a better person and would share my experiences with the world—after all, isn't that the kind of deal you are supposed to make when you are close to death? The only problem with that kind of deal is that I wasn't a bad person (yet) and since I was only five weeks shy of my fifteenth birthday, I didn't have a lot of experience to share with anyone, much less the world. So I tried to work out a different deal: *If God will let me live long enough to have some experiences, then...*

This wasn't making any sense. My mind grew increasingly fuzzy—and then the lights went out.

CHAPTER 2

Don't be a "Why Baby"

Ceiling lights flashed past, like in a subway tunnel, as they wheeled me into the operating room.

Doctors hovered over me, telling my mother it was probable that I would not survive the next few hours. They were as point-blank as the shot that paralyzed me.

Their words floated through my puzzled mind: *Paralyzed. Critical condition. Might not make it. Confined to a wheelchair if he lives.* It didn't make sense. *Why? Why? Why me? Why did my friend shoot me? I'm an athlete. I can't be paralyzed!* I did wonder why (sometimes I still wonder why). It didn't seem fair—*and it wasn't.*

I confess that I spent a fair amount of time asking why this happened—as anyone would—but at some point during those first few pain-ridden weeks, I came to the hard realization that it didn't matter "why." Asking that question repeatedly was futile. I needed to get on with healing and moving ahead with my life. Being a "why baby" wasn't helping.

But I'm getting ahead of my story. As I lay in the emergency room listening to the doctors announcing their grim predictions, I was bewildered and somewhat defiant. I was an accomplished athlete. I was a *quarterback.* I was Superman. Being paralyzed was a far greater concern in my young mind than even death. Before the championship game had started, my career as an athlete was over. Gone were the sports activities which were the passion of my life. Gone were the cheering crowds (and cute cheerleaders). Gone was the rush of competition—or so I thought.

This was real. I was on the brink of losing my life. If I did survive, I would likely spend the rest of my days in a wheelchair. I had never known anyone in a wheelchair. I imagined I would be institutionalized and never see my friends again. I could see myself in one of those big wicker chairs, sitting on a porch, kept warm with a lap robe knitted by church ladies, waiting to be fed by blue-haired nurses who were kind, but firm. "Come now, Michael, take another bite…" Live or die, this seemed like the end of everything for me.

My gaze remained locked on my mother's worried face until the door to the operating room swung shut leaving her standing silently in the hallway, tearfully praying for my life. I realized how much my mom loved me, and believed in me. Once again, her comforting presence helped me hang on to life and hope.

God grant me the serenity to accept the things I cannot change, the courage to change the things I can, and the wisdom to know the difference.

This is known as the *Serenity Prayer*. It is said to be written by theologian Reinhold Niebuhr in the 1930s. It is a thoughtful piece, but *how do we know what cannot be changed, without at least trying?* How do you know what cannot be changed without pushing the limits? Maybe it's okay to get a little frustrated at first—even a *lot* frustrated—*then* get serene!

Even though my *mood* was frightened and desperate, my *attitude*— the position I would operate from—began to shift. Even before the operating room doors swung closed I began to feel that everything somehow would be okay. It didn't make sense, it often doesn't, but it was how I felt—everything *would* be okay.

I don't know why I took this constructive view of things so quickly. Whether because of example from great parents or simply positive genetics, after the bullet impacted my spine, my mind did what it always did in a crisis. While this situation was of far greater significance than a dropped pass in the fourth quarter with a 200 pound linebacker charging at me, and though I was panicked and afraid, my mind quickly locked into position—the position that it would all work out okay. Maybe I could not change my circumstances, but I could change my mental position about those circumstances. By managing my attitude, maybe I could manage the situation.

I didn't know exactly what would happen, but I knew that somehow I would "land on my feet"—even if sitting in a wheelchair. It is that attitudinal position that got me through those critical first few hours, then through rehab, then on through the trials and troubles—and triumphs—we call "life."

You see, that is all that "attitude" really is—a position. Having a *good* attitude means we tend to operate from the position that everything will work out. Having a *bad* attitude means we tend to operate from the position that nothing will work out.

Are you tired of people telling you that you have a good attitude when you are happy, and when you are not happy, your attitude is crappy? I get this all of the time. When I am in a good mood I am called Happy Schlappi, and when I am in a bad mood I get called Crappy Schlappi. But that is my *mood*, not my *attitude*.

A mental attitude is a mental position, not a mood. You can be in a bad mood but have a good attitude. You can be in a good mood but have a bad attitude.

Sir Thomas More (who opposed King Henry's divorce from Catherine of Aragon) was likely not in a good *mood* when he was sentenced to the Tower of London to await execution for not agreeing with the King; but he certainly maintained a good (i.e. constructive, perceptive, enlightened) *attitude* or *position* relative to his incarceration—and that governed his behavior. Even through his eventual execution, he remained positive, resolute, and determined.

Was Sir Thomas More in a good mood the day of his execution? Probably not. But history reports that he remained calm and steadfast to the end, secure in his *position* that he was doing the right thing for the right reasons.

And I was secure, if not calm, in my position that somehow this would all work out. A week following the accident, I wrote my feelings

in the form of a poem. It isn't great poetry, but it reflects my constructive mind set, despite the pain I was in.

The Things We Have Lost

The things we've lost are the things that we love
But if we live good lives, we will regain them above.
Why things happen, God only knows
But what is planned for us, time only shows.
While we are waiting to find our spot,
We need to start working with what we have got.

We can take it easy or do the best we can,
That shows the difference between a boy and a man.
Where the path is rugged and the mountain steep,
What we learn here is ours to keep.
Where our vision stops is not the end,
There is a whole new world just around the bend.

By nature I have a good sense of humor; however, since being shot,
I hadn't yet laughed. What was there to laugh about? Nothing. Not
until Grandma Schlappi smuggled in a contraband 7-Eleven cherry
Slurpee!™

The night after writing the poem, I was moved from intensive care
into a regular hospital room. My grandmother was among my first
visitors.

She arrived late that night with the "illegal substance." She was determined to cheer me up by giving me the unauthorized treat. After
she left, the nurse came in to check my blood pressure and take my
temperature.

In those days they used a long, thin mercury thermometer that they
stuck under your tongue. You had to wait three to five minutes while the
silvery line slowly advanced to indicate your body temperature.

I decided to have some fun.

After the nurse left, I took the thermometer out of my mouth and stuck it into the remaining half of my cherry Slurpee.™ She hadn't noticed the contraband on my nightstand. When I heard her return, I quickly popped the thermometer back inside my mouth, flopped my head to the side, and held really still.

Since I had just been transferred out of intensive care, the nurse had strict orders to keep an eye on me. I was stable, but I still had a collapsed lung and a bullet lodged in my spine.

Gently taking the thermometer from my slack mouth, she took one look—and realized that I had died twenty degrees ago. In quiet hysteria she dropped the thermometer, grabbed for a pulse with one hand and for the emergency buzzer with the other. I held still as long as I could stand it; then suddenly burst out laughing. She was not amused. I was. Not only was I amused, I felt really alive for the first time since I had been shot.

I got a lecture. I listened carefully. I promised never to do those kinds of things anymore—I planned something even better.

This was the first time I had laughed since the accident. At that moment, I realized something that has often sustained me in tough times since. Although things may not always go as I would like, I could still retain my sense of humor and keep life in perspective. That laugh was a stepping-stone for me in the recovery process. I learned that I could still have as much fun as any other fourteen-year-old boy—but I would do it on wheels instead of gym shoes.

When I was finally transferred to the rehabilitation center in Salt Lake City, I saw a patient scooting along in the hallway, face down, on a flat, four-wheeled cart. He wasn't really looking where he was going. I realized that he was blind. I asked one of the attendants about him. He told me that he had been paralyzed in a car accident, and had become very depressed. Sinking ever deeper into depression and despair, he finally put a gun in his mouth and pulled the trigger. He didn't succeed in killing himself. Instead, he instantly lost his eyesight, leaving him more disabled than ever.

So, again "shot happened" to him. This time it was self-imposed; and now the man (Bob) was both paralyzed and blind. But for some reason this time when *shot* happened, *shift* happened. Bob's attitude shifted and he became one of the most cheerful, genuinely happy patients in rehab.

I didn't really understand "attitude" or "Attitude Therapy" or the idea that attitude was—or could be—a consciously chosen position, but for some reason Bob had adopted a much better position with regard to his circumstances than he had before he shot himself.

Bob was now physically in a facedown position, but in a much better mental and emotional position. He had a tough situation to deal with, but shifted his attitude and went scooting on through life. He was a great example to me.

I had aches and pains, but Bob helped me realize that I too would survive my circumstances and make a great life for myself. Bob's attitude reinforced my growing belief that all would be okay. This position was reinforced by a special visitor—an *almost* Heisman Trophy winner.

My mother's diary recorded the meeting:

Mike had a special visitor. Gifford Nielson, All-American quarterback. He told Mike of his own deep disappointment when he was favored to win the coveted Heisman Trophy, then his hopes were dashed when he injured his knee. He counseled Mike to make his life a practice of moving forward.

Gifford leaned forward over the bottom of the bed to shake Mike's hand. Mike leaned forward from the top of the bed, but he could barely touch Gifford's fingertips. Gifford's stiff knee and Mike's handicap prevented contact. Mike smiled and said, "Two handicaps don't work too well together even if you are moving forward." They both laughed.

Then there was Mike's first "roll model" Mike Johnson, who had lost both legs and the fingers of his left hand to an exploding land mine in Viet Nam. He came rolling in one day with his confident grin and casual stories of his wife and family and job and... his "normal" life. He gave my son hope and enthusiasm.

Randy Riplinger, a KUTV news reporter, asked my son what he was going to do in the future. Mike answered: "The same thing I would have done, but I'll do it differently."

After his transfer to Holy Cross, we stayed with Mike in his new room to make sure he was going to be okay. By Saturday the medics had stopped all of the pain medication. All of us were grateful that the pain in his back had subsided. But he was having problems with his eyes. His eyelids were heavy, they ached, and his vision was blurred. When nurses tried to put him in a wheelchair he endured it for about fifteen minutes then got very dizzy.

The tilt table, which automatically elevated him up and down to send blood to his feet and head, made him sick. The doctors told us that his reaction was common with injuries such as his.

By the following Tuesday when Grandma Palmer spent the day with Mike, we thought the turning point had come because he was feeling stronger and more stable. Harry James, University of Utah's tennis coach—who was also partially paralyzed—brought a tennis player with him and the three visited. James gave Mike some hand controls for his car to use when he could drive again. He also told Mike that everyone has some kind of handicap. "You just can't see the ones others have," he explained. He invited Mike to come and watch the U of U team work out. He promised that he would help him learn more about wheelchair tennis.

Friday after Thanksgiving Mike had a big workout day. The rehabilitation instructor had him climb into his chair by himself and he lifted weights in the physical therapy room.

When Saturday came and Mike's dad and I got to the hospital, he was popping "wheelies" in his wheelchair.

I met Mike's new roommate. Bert is about 27 and six feet tall. He had been in an industrial accident two months earlier and suffered brain damage. The medics operated and were giving him a better chance of recovery with marked improvement every day. He made Mike laugh so hard. Though his reactions and reflexes were very slow, he always came up with a witty answer in his slow monotone voice.

Mike played wheelchair basketball with him and the two of them laughed themselves silly.

How interesting it is that with all the medical help, and rehabilitation I received, it was a brain-injured man with a sense of humor and a benched quarterback with an attitude of positive expectation who would reawaken my focus, energy and drive. They started me on a wheelchair basketball career that would eventually take me to Olympic stadiums on four continents—and a professional speaking career.

As I wheeled myself out of the rehab center only six weeks after the shooting, I paused and looked at my world made new by my altered circumstances. I thought, *it feels weird to be in a wheelchair, and I don't really like it, but it's going to be a great life somehow.* That was, and is, my position—the attitude of positive expectation.

I was done being a "why baby."

CHAPTER 3

When Bullet Hits Bone

The bullet didn't break my back. So, what paralyzed me? It was shock—the shock waves that radiated through my body when bullet hit bone.

Have you ever felt defeated? Overwhelmed by a crushing loss that leaves you paralyzed—mentally, spiritually, or even physically? It isn't the circumstance that paralyzes you. It is the shock. Even though, technically, you have everything it takes to move, you can't because of the deep penetrating shock that leaves you feeling helpless and immobilized.

What do you do? It depends on your attitude. No, I don't mean it relies on being in a happy, snappy mood day in and day out. I mean it depends on deciding on and maintaining a constructive, determined will to survive, moving forward despite circumstances that may have you—for the moment—face down on the mat.

My wife Tami often says, "Things turn out best for the people who make the best of the way things turn out." My wife is pretty smart (she married me, didn't she)! I believe Coach John Wooden originated the phrase, or made it popular; but I think my wife is just as smart as he is—and certainly prettier—so maybe she said it first and he copied her! Anyway, it is a great quotation because it is true—and it works. The word "make" is key. "Things turn out best for those who *make* the best of the way things turn out." That implies a conscious decision and determination to act and react ("respond") differently than our mood might otherwise dictate.

You may recall that old trite statement *Mind over Matter*, or the equally trite but funny statement *Mind over Mattress*. I like to say, *Mind over Mood.* Not that the mind will necessarily govern our mood (though it can certainly affect it), but that we can decide to let the decisions of the rational mind govern our reactions and responses, rather than be dictated by the mood of the moment.

Many refer to logical or rational decisions as "left brain" decisions and emotional decisions as "right brain" decisions. Some refer to the left and right sides of the brain as male and female sides of the brain respectively—"male" being the logical or left side and "female" being the emotional or right side. I don't know how much truth there is to those theories, or how appropriate it is to identify such tendencies by gender, but it is important to recognize that we do have both logical and emotional responses to situations and that both are important.

Attitude and *mood* are often used interchangeably. They shouldn't be. The fact is, attitude is *not* an emotional response. It is not a mood. It is a position—consciously or unconsciously—sometimes passionately, sometimes dispassionately—that is chosen.

When you are emotionally upset and someone suggests that you have a bad *attitude*, what they usually mean is that you are in a bad *mood*. When they suggest that you change your *attitude*, what they usually mean is that you should change your *mood*. That's okay, except it can be difficult to just arbitrarily change your mood, and it is not always the healthiest thing in the world to disregard or manipulate one's own feelings or otherwise try to force a change in one's mood.

Your *mood* is an emotional reaction based on *circumstance*. Your *position* is a logical or rational decision based on *principle*. It is perfectly healthy to consciously and deliberately choose or change your position. You can be in a bad mood and still win—like Genghis Khan.

Character and integrity are a result of consciously setting standards (adopting a position) based on principles. I want more money and power, but I am not going to steal or cheat or hurt someone else in order to get it, even though the opportunity may be right in front of me. The consciously chosen position regarding that temptation overrules the desire or mood of the moment. An attitude of integrity might therefore be considered a position based on principle. I shouldn't steal (principle) therefore I won't steal (position). That is an attitude (position) of integrity.

Is it not, then, our position regarding circumstances that has the greater effect on our responses and, over the long haul, the outcomes we enjoy or suffer?

Moods can be all over the map because they are emotional reactions to circumstances, while attitudes or positions are more stable and constant because they are *responses* to situations. Responses are driven by reason based on principle.

Attitude is, therefore, simply a position we take relative to what is going on around us—our surroundings, circumstances, or environment. If I were writing a dictionary, I would define "attitude" like this:

at•ti•tude [at-i-tood, -tyood]
[noun] [Synonym: POSITION].
1. *Physical.* A position of the body illustrative or expressive of an action, emotion: a threatening attitude; a relaxed attitude. *(Rodin's "Thinker" presents a man in a thoughtful attitude.)*
2. *Ballet.* A dance position or pose. *(Her attitude was technically perfect.)*
3. *Aeronautics.* The inclination of the three principal axes of an aircraft relative to horizon, air current, etc. *(The pilot checked the attitude indicator to determine the exact tilt of the plane before deciding what action to take.)*
4. *Gen.* A physical, mental, financial, social, (etc.) tendency or position adopted or devised with regard to specific or general situations or circumstances; an orientation: *a negative attitude; a constructive attitude. (He had a positive attitude with regard to his incarceration. He took a positive position with regard to the economy.)*
Good attitude = the position that everything will work out.
Bad attitude = the position that nothing will work out.

As you may have surmised, I haven't actually authored a dictionary. This is the first word I have ever attempted to define. And in case I decide to write a dictionary, "A" is a pretty good letter to start with, right?

By the way, is "good" or "bad" appropriate verbiage to define one's attitude or position towards something or someone? Perhaps we would be better served if we used terms like "constructive" or "destructive," "friendly" or "unfriendly," "healthy" or "unhealthy."

You see, you can be in a good mood or a bad mood, but *attitudes* are not necessarily good or bad. Your position might be generally positive (everything is going to work out) or generally negative (nothing will ever work out). It is how we position ourselves as we move forward from day to day. It is the way we interpret or frame our existence. It involves what we perceive or interpret as victory or success and what we perceive as defeat or failure.

At the end of a ball game—one half of the audience is cheering while the other half is weeping. A war ends and one country cheers while the other mourns. Same outcome, just a different perspective, view, or interpretation—consequently a different mood.

Attitude, however, is not a mood. Attitude is a position. If I perceive that the desired outcome of an outing with my family is to have a memorable adventure—then it doesn't matter much if the sun shines and we all catch our limit of brook trout, or if it rains or snows, or the tent collapses in the middle of the night. If "shot happens" we will simply capture memories of the disaster so we can all have a good laugh as we look at the pictures later. By taking that positive position, nothing can ruin our vacation, short of excessive bleeding or loss of life or limb.

If I look at the adventure of climbing a mountain as worth the risk of falling—and then I do fall—I will more likely appreciate the adventure of the free fall, and the stitches and splints, and the healing process as simply a part of the thrill of the adventure. Well, you get the drift. It is our position and direction relative to our "disasters" that makes life a great experience or not.

Do you generally respond to tough circumstances or situations as if they will likely work out? Or do you react as though they won't? How is that serving you? If you generally approach life with the position that you will ultimately fail, I encourage you to try and shift your position just a bit and see if that serves you better. Don't try and force your mood, just shift your position—and see what happens.

Why is this distinction between *mood* and *attitude* so important? Because understanding it (and applying it) helps us establish better control—and fairly quickly—over our responses to (and consequently the outcomes of) the circumstances that affect our lives—even if we can't control the circumstances themselves. As my editor told me when I was writing this book, "Mike, you *transcend* your circumstances. No one sees what you deal with—the pain and frustration, the pins and needles of damaged nerves, the constant sciatica… well, Mike, sometimes we don't readily help you when you need a little assistance over an extra high curb or whatever because we forget that you are in a wheelchair. In fact, we lean on you (of course we have to lean down a bit) because of the way you show up. We don't see you as disabled or even "differently-abled" or "uniquely-abled" as the politically correct new-speak editors would have us say. We just see you as "Mike." Even-tempered, level, stable…"

Oh, if he had any idea how rotten a mood I am in sometimes! But he is right that my *attitude* is pretty even, pretty stable, even when my mood isn't. Moods are usually difficult to "snap out of" but attitudes or positions are more a matter of decision and choice. As I said earlier, we could paraphrase the old "Mind over Matter" as a way of making the best of things and say that our success is ultimately a result of exercising "Mind over Mood"

But how do we do that? How do we exercise "Mind over Mood?" The easiest way I know of is to recognize that we want to change—and give ourselves credit for that positive intent—then simply *decide* to take a different position toward difficult situations. We can take the attitude that things happen for a positive reason, or we can take the position that we can *create* a positive reason for why things happen. Either way, it works no matter what *mood* we are in at the time.

Clarifying the definition of "attitude" and understanding that it is a consciously chosen position and not a subjective mood, puts you in better control of your world. By adopting a constructive position regardless of your mood, you can help turn bad days into good days, and tough experiences into memorable experiences.

Earlier, I offered my definition of "attitude," emphasizing the idea that it is a position. What gives me the right to tweak the Queen's English—to define words the way I want to? What makes me the "attitude" expert? My life experience. Experience that resulted from my decision to choose my position with regards to my circumstances—and the wonderful life that resulted—gives me the right to at least have an opinion about it and offer something of what my life has taught me—something that works for me.

Others can agree or disagree with me, all or in part, and that's fine—and that's my attitude.

CHAPTER 4

A Mother's Diary

Friday, November 11, 1977—Veteran's Day. Michael was out of school today because of a Parent-Teachers Conference. About 2:30 p.m., he ran over to his friend Torrey Fetheroff's house. Mike was an All-Star Football player and he had gone over to get Torrey to practice for an important game.

About 3:00 p.m., the phone rang. I heard Torrey's voice yelling on the other end of the line, "Mrs. Schlappi, come quick, Mike's been hurt!"

"What's wrong?" I said, sensing that something in fact was very, very wrong,

Torrey replied, "Just hurry!" Then the line went dead.

I ran out of the door shouting to my sister, Janet, who was visiting: "Mike's been hurt. I've got to go!"

I jumped into the Suburban and drove to Torrey's house, which was only three houses to the north (why I drove, I'll never know). Torrey met me at the door telling me Mike was in the back bedroom. I ran to him and found him lying on the bed. He had his shirt pulled up exposing his chest. He said, "Mother, I've been shot! I can't breathe, and I can't move my legs."

My heart was in my throat. I had a terrible sick feeling. I told Mike to lie quietly, while I called the ambulance. Mike seemed alert and calm, in good control and that helped me think more clearly. Torrey was in shock, running through the house screaming, going out of his head. Mike kept calling out, "It's okay, Torrey, it's okay!"

I called the ambulance, but couldn't get Torrey settled enough to give me the exact house address. Janet had followed me on foot to see what was *happening and helped me figure out where we were, then we both stood by Michael to comfort him while we were waiting for the ambulance. I kept trying to figure out where the heart is located. Janet and I didn't want to move him because he had no feeling in his legs. I could hear Torrey screaming and tearing around the house.*

I was astonished at how fast help arrived. The first one through the door was a policeman—Torrey's father who was on duty at the time. Then came the paramedics, right on his heels. The first thing the paramedics did was to straighten Michael out on the bed and check his vital signs. They knew right away he had a collapsed lung. He was in a lot of pain by then, but was still cooperative. Quickly the medics got some oxygen into Mike and called for the stretcher.

Just then Michael's father, Larry, arrived and helped to put our son on the stretcher. I realized I was now in shock. They put Mike in the ambulance and asked us to ride in the police car. Richard Jones, the Bishop of our local congregation, rode with us. My daughter, Jennifer, who was only four, tried to grab me as we got in and finally a neighbor took her. I noticed a man there with a camera, a newsman I guess, and the street was filled with curious onlookers and concerned neighbors.

Though we moved quickly through traffic, the ride in the police car seemed to take forever. When we arrived at the hospital, Mike was already in the emergency room. They were treating his lung, ordering x-rays, watching his blood pressure and pulse. The admission clerks kept asking us questions. My husband and I couldn't even think.

Finally, the neurosurgeon, Dr. Kirkpatrick, arrived. He examined Michael, studied the x-rays and then tested him for feeling. There was no feeling at all from his waist down.

Mike began having terrific stomach cramps. My mother, Mary Palmer, arrived at the hospital at this time. Rex Skinner was also there. He was the detective assigned to the case. The surgeon made an incision in Mike's right side about four inches down from the armpit and inserted a tube to drain the blood from the lung and chest cavity.

The neurosurgeon finally called Larry and me into a side room and reviewed the x-rays with us. He showed us that it appeared the bullet had damaged the spinal column. Dr. Kirkpatrick was so blunt and cold with his facts, I just knew he couldn't be right, even though he explained in detail what the x-rays were showing. The general surgeon, who was friendlier, told us Mike's vital signs were fair but couldn't explain how the bullet missed Mike's heart, having taken the path that it did. We were told by the doctors that if Mike could hang on in intensive care for the next 24 to 36 hours, he would have a good chance of making it.

I never knew I could ever love a child so much as I did at that moment. I wanted to do anything I could to help him. The next time we talked to the neurosurgeon, he told us he had told Mike he might never walk again. When I heard this I thought how cruel to tell a young boy who was desperately fighting for his life that he may be disabled for life if he did survive.

The doctor also told us that there was one chance in a million that Mike could recover use of his legs if feeling returned to them within three or four days. He explained that when a bullet is involved, the intensity of the shock wave to the body could paralyze, even if the spinal cord wasn't severed.

After that consultation, we knew it would take a miracle for Mike to walk again. We tried to understand. Why? Why Mike? Why did this happen to us—to Mike?

Finally, we were able to ask Mike what really happened. The story Torrey had related was different from the real truth. The version we heard on the radio when we were riding in the police car was that Mike's wound was self-inflicted. Of course, his dad and I both knew Mike had been taught well about gun safety. But after hearing Mike's own story when he was strong enough to tell us, we knew Torrey had not told the truth. We were certain it was simply the desperate act of a boy afraid to admit to his policeman father that he'd been careless with his father's off-duty pistol.

Torrey had told his dad that Mike shot himself when he tried to put the gun in the nightstand. We knew that was false because Mike was lying at the top of the bed unable to move his legs and the pistol and bullets were resting on the bottom of the bed five feet from Mike.

We told Detective Skinner the real story and Torrey finally tearfully admitted the truth. He badly needed to get the heavy burden of his lie off his chest.

What made Mike's father and I feel good was the knowledge that Mike harbored no feelings of hatred for his good friend. His father and I never really felt any anger for the boy either, knowing that a human error had been committed and so often the innocent are the ones to suffer.

Saturday, the day Mike was supposed to play in the football game with Torrey, he was still stabilizing after a long night of careful monitoring. The physicians had placed a tube in his right lung to drain the blood and watch for internal bleeding. His stomach was beginning to ache with awful pain. The doctor explained that his nervous system had been so shocked that it was now super sensitive. Mike was given a Demerol (Meperidine) shot every four hours. It gave him relief for an hour or two and then wore off. It was so bad that he screamed if his stomach was touched even by a bed sheet.

Mike appreciated how terrific the intensive care nurses were at Utah Valley Hospital. They were understanding and went out of their way to make him more comfortable.

By Saturday night, Mike was alert enough to watch Brigham Young University play Arizona State in a contest to decide the Western Athletic Conference (WAC) football title. The game goes on, and so does life. That's my boy. Mike was moved across the hall so he could watch the game on TV. We sat with him until we knew he was tiring.

After I was discharged from the hospital, my mother brought me her diary and let me read what she wrote about those early days of trauma and recovery. My mother's diary not only clarifies the sequence of events following the shooting, but also helps me recall my feelings about the incident that altered my life so drastically. I discovered something important about those of us who are seriously injured.

When the injury is extreme, the healing process can completely absorb you. Later, you remember the process in general, but forget most of the details. You remember especially the shock of the initial impact of the situation, whether it is a physical injury as in being shot or an emotional injury from divorce or death. When *shot* happens, shock happens; and the pain relieving chemicals released protect us from pain and future pain by masking the memory.

I not only learned a lot about the recovery process from my mother's daily journal, I also learned how important it is to have family and friends who show their love and support—and more importantly their acceptance and respect. Mom put it this way:

"I can't begin to acknowledge the gratitude I felt for the people who made Mike's recovery a priority in their lives, and I thought to myself again and again how insignificant everything I was doing prior to Mike's accident. After all, people are the most important thing here on this earth; and how we learn to help other people must be the main plan of our Father in Heaven.

Sunday and Monday Mike was able to eat a little bit. He was given liquids the first two days. A pain in his back caused great concern. The doctor explained that it came from the injury caused by the bullet damaging nerves. He cautioned us that the pain could last two weeks, two months, or forever.

Dr. Gaufin, the neurosurgeon now treating Mike, answered our questions and explained the medical aspects of what had happened to him. He told us that if Mike continued to progress as well as he is, he could be moved from Intensive Care on Tuesday, and on Friday, he should be transferred to Holy Cross Hospital in Salt Lake City. There, rehabilitation would begin.

Dr. Gaufin also informed us that every hour that passed without sensation returning to his legs, the chance of Mike regaining the use of them was reduced.

Tuesday, Mike was moved to a regular room. He was so glad to have a phone and enjoyed talking to his friends. He was delighted when one of his favorite teachers, Paul Gourdin, and fifteen of his classmates came to his room. They hung a poster on the wall with everyone's signature written on it. It was about eight feet tall. Mail was pouring in for Mike. The student council brought Mike a plant in a basketball planter. That night kids from his school flocked into his room. So many, in fact, that the nurse reported they were jamming the elevators and crowding the halls.

It was a great treat for Mike because he loved his friends and they certainly showed their feelings for him. They brought cards, flowers, candy, games and Mike's spirits soared when he was with them.

Mike lifted everyone's spirits with his attitude. I know I always felt better when I was with him.

They say everyone has fifteen minutes of fame. I actually had fifteen *days* of fame—but now it was over. I was no longer front-page news. Two weeks after a dramatic life-altering event that captured the hearts of the entire community, I was old news. My family was still with me and they always would be. I still had my close friends who came to see me as often as they could, but they had their lives, and I understood that. There was an occasional bit of media coverage about some aspect of what had happened, but reality was setting in and I knew I was pretty much on my own.

That is the way of almost all situations: divorce, death, depression, etc. Your friends gather around supportively then, before you even get used to the loss, they are on about their lives. That isn't good or bad; it's just the way it is. It is important to realize this, because it is our attitude, *our* position toward our circumstances—not our friends—that makes the difference in the long haul.

They transferred me to the rehabilitation center where I began my therapy (physical and occupational therapy, personal functionality and sexuality, emotional and physical pain management, etc.). As I went through the exercises and training that would help me adjust, survive and ultimately succeed, I had ample time to reflect on how good my life had been. I also realized something else that was really important. I realized that life was *still* good.

Does that make sense? How could life be good? I was not even fifteen years old and had become a "has been" athlete. I was confined to a wheelchair, my athletic career over before it started, my entire sense of self was turned upside down. Two weeks ago I was student body president, a popular young athlete and now I wondered if girls would like me or if my friends would even remember me.

So, "life is *good*?" Really? How does that make any sense? Well, life was—and is—good because I had the good fortune to be raised by good parents.

Author Og Mandino asks a significant question:

How many parents, in moments of anger, push the "kill" switch on one of their kids by telling their little boy or girl that he or she will never amount to anything? How many kids then spend a lifetime working very hard to make their parent's prophecy come true?

That does *not* describe *my* parents. My mom and dad were an incredible support system. They had already instilled in me the attitudes that would carry me through this nightmare into a new day—a future that would prove more productive and positive than I could have ever imagined. Please understand, they didn't *become* supportive after my accident, they *already were supportive*. The way they raised us had already imbedded in my bones the belief that I could overcome anything.

Actually I had *better* overcome *everything* because there were chores to be done! My mom was gentler, but my dad—well his theme was, "Get over it and get on with it!"

CHAPTER 5

Get Over It and Get On With It

I was one of seven children, but I always knew that I was important. I also knew I could accomplish anything I set my mind to. As trite as that sounds, it was true. I believed it. My parents believed in me—as they believed in all of their children. Therefore, I believed in myself.

Instead of getting lost in a big family, all of us kids were recognized as being important and significant; hence, jealousy and rivalry were minimized and mutual support and teamwork were enhanced. Everyone excelled in something. Teamwork, not competition, was a natural result—even though we were very competitive outside the family.

My brother, Scott, was a little older than I—fifteen months to be exact. He was stronger, stable, calm—even cautious. I was a crazy risk taker who lived life on the edge. He stabilized me; I loosened him up.

Scott included me in his life, rather than treat me like a bothersome little brother. When I was ten years old, I played on the Dodgers Little League baseball team. Scott, without question the best baseball player in the city, was the star pitcher and I was the catcher. We won the city championship. This was the first time I thought of myself as a champion. I'll always remember that feeling. It would never have happened without my big brother treating me like a team player instead of just a little brother.

Scott was the role model I always found myself trying to live up to, striving and stretching, extending myself beyond my limits. Though just a kid himself, he was a great teacher who took time to lift me to his level. We had sibling rivalry, to be sure, but much of my progress, both as an athlete and as a person, I owe to Scott.

He was a special inspiration to me during my recovery. It was the best thing he could do for me. We had always been the "Schlappi Boys," joined at the hip. Two little star athletes growing up in the community—then I got shot. I was no longer an athlete (so I thought). I was a "has-been" sitting by myself on the upper tier of the bleachers, in the wheelchair section, wishing I was down there with my brother.

This isn't any fun. Why did my friend shoot me? I'm having a bad day.

That became my bad mood mantra when things went wrong: *This isn't any fun. Why did my friend shoot me? I'm having a bad day.*

You will hear me say it even now when my wheelchair is stuck in the slushy, dirty snow next to my car when the handicap stall has been taken by some thoughtless dweeb; or I can't reach a new roll of toilet paper on the top shelf and no one is around to help. *"This isn't any fun. Why did my friend shoot me? I'm having a bad day."*

If you get anything out of this book, please get this: It's okay to have a bad day. When "shot happens," it is okay to say, "I am miserable, sad, mad, frustrated, angry, depressed, disillusioned…" If that is your mood, if that is how you feel, acknowledge it—at least to yourself. Just don't let your bad mood become your operating position.

Our family went snowmobiling, hunting, fishing, played ball, went to sports events, had family vacations and more. We did things together. We also were encouraged to excel on our own, and excel we did! In the years that followed, my younger sister, Julie, became an all-state basketball player and served on the student council. She was my "private nurse" after my accident. Collette was a two-sport athlete; however, music was her first love. She became Little Miss Utah when she was eight years old (yes, she was adorable). Jennifer played high school basketball and became a collegiate athlete. Todd was also a basketball player and an Eagle Scout like his brothers. Tyler was the starting guard on a state championship high school basketball team.

Everyone was an athlete and we all played musical instruments. Good grades were expected—and achieved.

My dad was the high school basketball coach. He was also my personal coach. He was tough, but he had blessed me with DNA that made me equal to the task, so it worked for me. When I made a bad shot, got a bad break, skinned my knee, he made certain that *his* mantra resounded in my ears, "Get over it, son—and get on with it."

I loved going to the gym with Scott and Dad. Nothing could be greater than a good game of basketball. I was a gym rat from day one and, because I had a competitive bulldog nature, there wasn't anything I couldn't do with a ball in my hands. It was cool to be the son of a coach. It was cool to be the brother of a champion. It was cool to be cool.

Playing sports was the most natural way for us to spend our time. We loved to fish and hunt and play night games behind the nearby church. The thread of "competing" and being my very best was woven into my personal fabric. It became me, no matter what the endeavor. I had a natural talent for athletics and was always called out first to be on a team. Once chosen, it seemed always to fall on me to lead and direct the team. I loved the challenge.

Our family environment was designed to encourage success, whatever "success" meant to the individual. This was my "success" and my family reveled in the fact that I reveled in it. I am certain they would have been just as supportive no matter what it was—as long as it wasn't illegal or fattening!

What about work? Work was important. No matter what you did around the house, with a family that size, it was meaningful—no matter how menial the chore. We had a large family and it took the efforts of each one of us to take care of all the chores. Hard work—even menial work—as well as living high ideals and achieving personal potential were core family values.

Now that I was dealing with a disability, finding new meaning in my life (or redefining "old meaning") was critical to my recovery and success, and I had just the family to help me find it. My dad's consistent, though sometimes unspoken, admonition, "Get over it and get on with it," was a constant. So I did get over it and I did get on with it. My parents made sure of it.

Before my accident, I was given a list of chores to do weekly and I checked them off daily.

After my accident I was given a list of chores to do weekly and I checked them off daily.

My parents taught me that life didn't change, despite the fact *circumstances* change—sometimes drastically.

I still had to weed a row in the garden weekly, change broken sprinkler heads, do the dishes, and whatever other tortures my parents could inflict on me right along with all their other six children. Nothing really changed. Only how I did it changed.

When the family picked pears, I sat on the plastic tarp under the tree and sorted the fruit—big pears from little pears—and ducked—a lot! I did my part in the daily routine of setting the table before a meal and washing the dishes afterward. I stacked the dirty dishes in my lap, wheeled them from the dining room to the kitchen, then sat sideways against the sink and rinsed them off before putting them in the dishwasher. I hated it. Not because I was in a wheelchair, but because I was a normal 15 year old boy!

Once in a while I enjoyed an advantage. One year we acquired handcarts and spent our family vacation trekking over the Wasatch Mountains in Utah, as did our ancestors. I lay in the cart like an injured pioneer. We all have our jobs; this time, mine was the easiest! When my brothers complained that they had to pull or push and all I had to do was sit there with fake bandages, I would smile and say (mimicking my dad as best I could) "c'mon, get over it and get on with it!" My dad never said a word—he just grinned!

Most of my friends (except those who just faded away) treated me as though nothing had happened. I think it was because my friends and family treated me so normally, that it wasn't so hard on me when others moved out of my life. For the most part, my friends included me as they always had. I especially appreciated friends like Christa, Russell, Phil, Doug, Roger, Wendy, Matt, Jana (I hesitate to name names because there were so many) and their families. There wasn't anything they wouldn't do for me. They were especially supportive after my accident and I owe them a great deal.

My teammates and friends became my cheerleaders and my peer coaches. They included me. They not only made certain that I got involved and stayed involved, they also treated me as if I was still me—which I was—and am.

I went cruisin' with them just like anyone else. They would throw me into the backseat and toss the wheelchair in the trunk. They'd drive to the local McDonalds, run in and order their Big Mac's and fries, eat and flirt with the girls—and forget that Mikey was still stuck in the car with his chair in the trunk.

But I liked it. (Yes, Mikey liked it!) They never forgot me; they just forgot that I was disabled and that made me feel normal.

A year following my accident, Torrey and I were hanging out at the local mall. It seemed that everyone who passed looked at me with a curious eye. I wanted to wear a t-shirt that reads: "I got shot. What's your problem?"

A lady once bluntly asked me why I was in a wheelchair. I simply and truthfully said, "Because my friend here shot me." He and I laughed. She didn't.

She wasn't trying to be rude or insensitive; she was simply curious. I had come to understand that the way I regarded myself and my circumstances would influence heavily the way others would regard me. They would either see me as a disabled paraplegic or a confident kid with pretty girlfriends, a cool car and a bright future.

My college friend, Doug Jensen, and I wanted to have some fun on a blind double date—at the expense of our dates—so I loaned him one of my wheelchairs and we both went "wheeling" up to the girls dorm to pick up our dates. We were not only blind dates, we were also paraplegics!

The girls politely avoided comment and went with us to the university bowling alley (wondering how these two could possibly bowl). On our way down the hill, bad luck struck! Not being practiced in the art of piloting a wheelchair, Doug lost control of his chair and landed directly in a window well. People came to his rescue and pulled him out (he just lay there feigning helplessness—the dweeb). Then we continued on to campus. Once there, Doug continued his charade by bowling from his chair, just as I did—until he again fell out of the chair.

Before the girls could come to his rescue, he jumped to his feet, yelling, "I'm healed!"

We're not sure our two dates enjoyed the experience, but we certainly did. Except for one thing: it took my date the rest of the evening to be convinced that I actually couldn't get out of mine.

One other friend I should mention is Skipper—my dad's hunting dog. He was my pal. He was my dad's dog according to Dad, but my dog according to me (besides, Skipper liked me best—because I fed him).

Skipper brought me my first painful experience with significant change when I was five years old. He was a playful energetic Springer spaniel with boundless energy and limitless personality. He was also an incorrigible car chaser.

I heard the screech of rubber on asphalt and the simultaneous "thump" and one sharp final, "Yike!" and Skipper was no more. I had never lost anyone before—or anything for that matter. My mom told me I would see him in heaven, but that seemed unreal and so far away. It did little to change the fact that facts could change.

Skipper's death affected me deeply. For the first time in my young life, I realized that things wouldn't always be the same. No matter how important something seemed, you could lose it. It wasn't easy, but I knew what I had to do. I had to—that's right—"Get over it and get on with it."

CHAPTER 6

This Should Only Happen
to Chess Players

Let's return to the hospital.

Those questions about my future chased each other about in my head as I slowly healed. Will my friends still accept me? Will my teammates still see me as an athlete—their quarterback or team captain—one of them—or just some guy in a wheelchair? Will girls like me? (A few days after the shooting accident, my girlfriend dumped me.) Will I ever get a normal job? Will they send me to some special home where I will sit in the sun with a blanket over my lap feeding the pigeons…

Well, I was a kid—and I was scared!

Though the thought of cute nurses giving me lots of attention held a certain attraction, I dreaded the thought of bland hospital food being served to me on plastic trays for the rest of my life.

Even more troubling were the basic questions that played through my mind like a scratched record (broken records don't play): *Why did God let this happen? Does He love me? Does He even care what happens to me?*

My mantra kicked in: *"This isn't any fun. Why did my friend shoot me? I'm having a bad day."* I guess I was pretty normal, right? Don't you also feel that way when "shot happens?"

I didn't think about the other approximately 10,000 people who become paralyzed every year from accident or illness (mostly males between the ages of eighteen and twenty-four—primarily from automobile accidents and gunshot wounds—see, shot happens a lot!). I could only think about me. I was young and from a small country town. I had never known or even seen a paraplegic, other than on the rare occasion when I saw a disabled person getting pushed around the mall in a wheelchair (with a blanket on his lap… etc.). Usually it was an older person, not a fifteen-year-old athlete.

"Why me?" I thought. "I need my legs—these things should only happen to chess players!"

If I really knew what was ahead of me, I would have been terrified—or despondent. Being paraplegic is much more than an issue of walking or playing sports. Few have any idea of what problems paralysis really brings. I certainly didn't.

Imagine trying to dress, go to the restroom, wash dishes (not that I ever wash dishes!), drive your car, etc. while lifting or dragging two thirds of your body weight—dead weight—that is non-responsive and imbalanced. Try it sometime. Try getting you *and a wheelchair* into your car without using your legs or lower back, or try getting onto a toilet seat—and staying there!

There is more to it than just that—as if that alone was not enough. There is also the problem of "electronic communication." When the spinal cord is compromised, it is like blowing out the central trunk line of a complicated telecommunications system. Eventually some signals get rerouted and stabilized so you can function, but your body never works quite right—and the pain is constant.

What pain? You'd think that if you are paralyzed and numb you wouldn't feel pain—but you do. Three-fourths of my body was (and still is) paralyzed and numb. But I was (and still am) in significant and constant physical pain. My back always hurts where the bullet lodged in my spine. I also have phantom pain. (Why do they call it "phantom pain?" Phantoms aren't real—but this pain sure is.) The nerves in my belly, legs, hips and side constantly feel like pins and needles are sticking in them. It is like how your foot feels "waking up" after it has been "asleep"—only more painful. I not only experience shooting pains and shocks, but there is that hot, irritating, tingle that just drives you around the bend.

In addition, there is a band around my middle (about five inches wide at the level where the bullet impacted my spine) that is only partially numb. The nerves are hypersensitive. The pain is constant and distracting. My body has varying degrees of numbness (if they were to make a movie of my life it would be entitled "Numb and Numb-er"). I could be the nation's #1 consumer of ibuprofen and other pain-killers if I wasn't afraid they would alter my already charming personality.

In fact, as we were writing this, my son Joseph (who is on my edit team) overheard my editor and me talking about this. Joseph was surprised to learn how much pain I feel every day. My son had no idea—and he lives with me!

In my keynote speeches, I say, "Only when you feel pain do you change and only when you change do you grow."

I just left them to work on this while I go stretch out for ten minutes because this "phantom pain" is so intense.

Now I am back and found out my editor only wrote two sentences while I was gone.

You just can't get good help these days!

My *mood* is disappointed, maybe even grumpy; but my *position* is to forge ahead with the book regardless.

Being unable to do simple chores like taking out the garbage or mowing the lawn without expending a ton more time and energy than the next guy—or my wife or kids—is frustrating, but I do it anyway as long as it needs to be done. That is my position. That is not always a position easy to maintain. If *you* are going to take the garbage out and it has been raining or the sprinklers have been on, it is no big deal, but for *me* it is a real project. I have to put the garbage on my lap then, with wet hands, negotiate a $3,000 wheelchair through a soft lawn while the rain and mud—well, you get the idea.

Then there are the *really* personal issues involving sexual and emotional intimacy. I know people wonder about them, but they rarely ask. These and other private issues—especially those that relate to my male ego—are difficult to address from the stage and I don't talk about them much. Besides, I don't want to seem like I am looking for sympathy.

It is important to understand how paralysis (of any sort) really affects one's life—especially as we make the distinction between how we "feel" about a situation and what our "attitude (position)" about it is—and what we do about it.

And what *do* we do about it? What do we do about the challenges and opportunities of life? As I have said, we do what everyone else does, (or wishes they could do). In the case of physical paralysis, you just do it differently. In this case, different isn't always bad, it's just different.

Some things are more than difficult, they are painful—but you just live with them (it beats the alternative!).

There is one thing you can do when the philosophizing fails—you can laugh! I really like what my editor says (my friend and fellow speaker, Brad Barton, quotes him in his book *Beyond Illusions*):

> *"No matter how terrible the tragedy or how great the disaster, it is heavily outweighed by the lessons learned, the growth experienced, and the wonderful stories told."*

I like to tell about my friend and Olympic teammate Reggie Colton, a double amputee who lost his legs in a train accident. When we fly, he loves to climb, like a spider monkey, into the overhead luggage bins on airplanes and scare the wits out of passengers when they stow their carry-ons (and you think paraplegics have bladder problems!).

Simple things can become complicated and undoable. Life can be like having limited cash trying to keep up with someone with a gold card. It is hard to prove your manhood when your wife can take out the garbage, change a light bulb, or mow the lawns quicker and easier than you can. Health and life insurance are very difficult to get. Statistically, paralysis shortens the lives of paralytics. I won't likely live as long as you will. (In a sense, I was actually shot to death.) It is difficult to adjust to a lot of things—and some things you never really adjust to, you just deal with them.

Some people wonder how I can joke about personal and sensitive issues of intimacy, incontinence, etc., but humor is a very important coping mechanism.

There are, of course, silver linings to the clouds. I couldn't play the piano any more. I told my mom I could no longer use the pedals. She bought it. It was almost worth getting shot, just to get out of piano lessons.

That was about the only concession I ever got from my parents, though. As you can see from earlier chapters, my family had the audacity to actually treat me as if I were normal.

Do you mind if I revisit our discussion about "attitude"? After all, that is what this book is about. As a young athlete, a word I used to hear—a lot—was "attitude." Now that I was in this rather tough situation, I wondered what my coach would think. I wondered if he would think I had a "good" attitude.

Then I wondered what "attitude" really meant.

I remembered my coach in the locker room enthusiastically telling us to get a *positive attitude* and we would win. I knew he would tell me that if I wanted to get through this I needed to have a good attitude. I wasn't in a very good mood, frankly. I worried that I would fail. I thought having a good *attitude* was the same as being in a good mood.

I was wrong.

I learned that attitude isn't a mood, it is a method—a method one could apply anytime, simply by being committed to doing it regardless of how one might feel at the moment.

I was in mental pain with the worries and uncertainty of my future, but I wasn't in despair. I had a positive mental attitude. I had PMA in my DNA; inherited from my naturally resourceful positive parents. (Remember "attitude" is "position" so maybe we should say I had PMP in my DNA but then it wouldn't rhyme.)

In addition to the intentional constructive mental and emotional conditioning provided by my parents in the course of my growing up, some of my positive positioning to my situation came from my sports training. For example, when you suffer a sports injury, they usually don't take you off the team, you are just benched temporarily—put on the "disabled list" until you recover. They expect you to recover then return to the field—and you usually do. In fact, if the injury isn't really disabling and wouldn't be exacerbated by continuing to play, good coaches often literally make you play through the pain.

What is your mood? Irritated and in pain. But what is your attitude or position? You play anyway—regardless of your mood—and you play to win.

My athletic coaches taught me almost exactly what my parents taught me. It was okay to have a bad day or a bad game, but it is not okay to have a bad life. It is okay to be in a negative mood sometimes, but it is not okay to maintain a negative position.

That combination of good parents and good coaching created in me that constructive approach to what was happening to me and what I was ultimately going to do about it (and gain from it). I am not sure I was clearly aware of what was in my mind during those critical first weeks. All I know is that I did not respond by going through the normal grief cycle of denial and despair (okay, maybe a little despair) before beginning the healing process.

Therapists warned my parents that I would have occasional screaming fits of frustration as I adjusted to my circumstances; but I never did. I just stayed fit, rather than *have* a fit. I had found out about wheelchair sports. Maybe I wouldn't have to play chess to be a world champion. Maybe I could be an accomplished athlete after all.

I knew my father felt deep frustration and sometimes real anger toward my friend, Torrey. Dad had high hopes for me as an athlete. As time went by, however, he not only accepted the situation, he maintained his position that (somehow) I would still be a great ballplayer. He did not know how, but he believed it possible. Isn't that a great expression? "He believed it possible." Not he believed it *was* possible; rather, *he believed it possible*. Like believing something so strongly it became possible. My dad planted seeds of promise in my mind that I could still be an accomplished athlete. I began then, to also "Believe it Possible."

CHAPTER 7

The Fate of Flight X

The late model passenger jet airliner taxied down the tropical runway, revved its engines and climbed steeply into the evening sky. The sun hung blood-red on the horizon as it prepared to sink into its nightly slumber in the sea. The 230 assorted passengers gazed out the windows, chatted casually with their seatmates, or fell asleep as the airliner banked in a long sloping upwards curve rising rapidly to 14,000 feet, then modified its climb to a slower ascent to cruising altitude.

Its heading was now east, away from the setting sun. What lay between it and its intended destination was calm air, a mountain range and clouds. Lots of clouds. Thick, heavy clouds. Dark clouds. Blackout.

But that was of little concern. This was a routine flight on a regular flight path. The late model jet airliner was in excellent condition. In addition, it had been recently re-outfitted and, in the process, new equipment had been installed, including a state-of-the art electronic attitude indicator.

No, I didn't say an "*altitude* indicator," which is an altimeter. I said "*attitude* indicator." "What's an attitude indicator?" Well, at the risk of insulting your intelligence, the attitude indicator does exactly that—it indicates the attitude of the plane. NASA refers to it as an ADI (Attitude Direction Indicator).

Wait. Attitude? Does a plane have a mood? I mean, can airplanes get grouchy and grumpy, and start out in the morning coughing and belching smoke and demonstrating a negative attitude like my granddad's old persnickety tractor? No, that is a mood.

A plane doesn't have a mood, but it does have an attitude—its position in relation to the horizon or ground during flight. While climbing the nose is pitched upward; while cruising it's mostly level; and while descending its pitched downward. Attitude also includes right and left roll (turn and bank), and yaw (side-to-side). Because I'm in a wheelchair, I am the first passenger on the plane and the last to get off. As a result, I have lots of opportunities to talk to pilots. It is unanimous. According to every commercial airline pilot I've consulted, the attitude (not *altitude*) indicator is the most important instrument in the plane's cockpit.

More important than the altitude indicator (altimeter)? Yes. Fuel gauge? Yes. Why? It is the primary instrument reference for all take-offs and landings, and continuously informs the pilot and copilot of the aircraft's position in the air. The instrument is essential, because commercial airline pilots can't always see the horizon or ground to visually determine their aircraft's attitude. At night or during zero visibility, the attitude indicator is essential to safe flying. Without it, specifically during zero visibility conditions, the pilot and copilot cannot tell if their aircraft is flying straight and true, banking left or right—or in a spiral dive toward the ground.

The attitude indicator is, therefore, directly in the line of sight of both the captain and the first officer—pilot and copilot. Each has two, not one, attitude indicators on separate circuits in case any or all of the others fail. Each has its own power supply—and the backup gyro attitude indicator has its own separate independent battery-backup as well. That is how vital the attitude of the plane is and the instrument that measures it. Even if all other instruments fail, expert pilots can navigate the plane to a safe landing with only the battery powered backup attitude indicator.

The plane in this story (based on an actual incident—unfortunately, not the only one of its kind) had that new, state-of-the-art, super-duper electronic attitude indicator so the pilot and copilot could tell what the plane's position was relative to the horizon. But it didn't have the backup that we have today. The new attitude indicator was backed up—but only by the old attitude indicator that had not been removed. The old one was, however, lower on the console and not directly in the line of sight of the pilots—as they are today.

You see, sometimes when you're in the air, blasting along in excess of 450 miles per hour, you don't really feel the roll when your plane is gradually turning because the centrifugal force keeps the coffee in the cups and the laptops on the laps. Something may not feel exactly right, but nothing seems exactly amiss either.

Please keep in mind, as I share this story about the fate of Flight X, that an airplane's *altitude* is how high it is measured from sea level. The plane is literally "up in the air." Clouds, wind, air pockets, turbulence—its environment is completely fluid, ever changing, just like our lives.

What began as an uneventful flight was about to became an eventful and fateful flight. At first everything was fine. The plane operated perfectly; the pilot and copilot were on top of their game. The flight attendants delivered their snacks and beverages and dealt with all the details that make for a comfortable trip.

They delivered coffee to the copilot. The captain didn't need anything at the moment. He was looking at a wall of thick clouds just ahead. They were beautiful. Heavy charcoal-black, trimmed in gold, red and pink from the setting sun behind the plane. The cabin darkened as the plane nosed into the clouds and the pilots lost all visual reference to the horizon and ground.

Shortly afterward, something went wrong—just a little. The attitude indicator showed the plane was banking slightly to the left. No problem. The pilot made a slight correction to apparently return the plane to level flight. I say "apparently" because—well, let's just stay with the story.

Soon the attitude indicator showed another slight bank to the left. Mildly curious, the pilot glanced over the other instruments, but not the old attitude indicator, which was not directly in his line of vision. All seemed okay, so he simply corrected again to the right without saying anything.

But the copilot noticed something. The coffee in his cup was not exactly level.

The plane was immersed in the bank of thick clouds. The conditions were mostly a blackout; the pilots couldn't see what was happening outside of their aircraft. The plane was on the correct path, but its position (its attitude) was tilted—slightly—like my wheelchair when one tire goes flat.

The captain was confused at the obvious discrepancy in the electronic attitude indicator and his copilot's coffee. So he decided to ascend to gain some safety in altitude while they sorted out the problem. He was, after all, flying over a high mountain range. It wouldn't do to clip a tree or a hunk of ice with a wing tip.

So he pitched the plane a few degrees upward and accelerated just a bit. Only he didn't fly exactly upward as he thought. The coffee was right. The state-of-the-art attitude indicator was wrong. The plane was immediately a few degrees off course, but the acceleration created additional centrifugal force that leveled the coffee in the cup and made it all seem right—but it wasn't. The plane was not just headed at an upward angle; it was headed in a slight upward *arc*, veering to the right and, though only slightly, it was now off course.

What the captain failed to do was check his old standby manual attitude indicator, which would have agreed with the coffee and told him to ignore the electronic indicator and level the plane.

The pilot had corrected the situation, but *with the wrong attitude.* He had therefore not corrected anything at all. He had actually made the situation worse. The plane now had a terrible attitude and was headed for disaster.

Now the pilots knew something was amiss—but they didn't know what. The gauges simply didn't agree with each other. Every few moments the malfunctioning electronic attitude indicator would indicate an increase in left tilt and the captain would again correct to the right.

Attempting to maintain a modest upward climb, the captain was actually veering the aircraft into an accelerating spiral that tightened with every "correction" until the plane ultimately began to spiral out of control; down—not up as the pilot and copilot thought—at full speed toward the ground.

For how long the centrifugal force held the pilots and the passengers in their seats—and the coffee in the cups—is unknown. When, if ever, the pilots figured out what the conflict between their instruments represented, is also unknown. However, they must have known at some point that they weren't climbing, but were in fact spiraling toward the earth at full throttle.

The airliner went from cruising speed to excessive speed and then spiraled out of control at over 600 miles per hour—straight for the jungle floor.

The record does not show when the captain or the copilot or the crew understood what was happening—or if they ever did. What they may have tried to do to correct the problem obviously didn't work.

Soon there was nothing left of "Flight X" except a smoking crater. Investigators on the scene were appalled. The wings and the tail had cracked from metal fatigue and ripped off. The fuselage was compromised, windows blown out, passengers and seats and luggage sucked out. Bodies were hanging in trees and wreckage was scattered over several square miles.

You have heard it said, *"Your Attitude Determines Your Altitude,"* and *"Attitude is Everything."* These euphemisms were first unique then popular (then eventually trite) because they were interesting, fun, and had a nice ring to them. They are poetic and alliterative. That is why they are so often used by motivational speakers, writers and publishers of posters of sandstone cliffs, sunsets, and hang-gliders.

They are also pretty much true. The attitude or position of the plane is the primary factor that affects the airplane's likelihood of achieving altitude.

It's the same with us. Our position is everything. Regardless of our mood—happy or irritated, grumpy or enthusiastic—our *position* can remain stable and constructive. Where moods tend to establish themselves because of immediate circumstances, or recent experience (sometimes we even wake up in a bad mood because of a dream we've had that hasn't a flake of reality to it), our moods are not typically a matter of choice, but our attitudes are. We can choose what position we will take toward our circumstance regardless of the mood we may be in.

"Attitude" isn't just a word used by motivational speakers and parents of grouchy teenagers. "Attitude" is a critically important element of a successful airplane flight—and a successful life. The position we take relative to our environment and circumstances—everything going on around us—makes the difference between achieving cruising altitude, or drilling a hole in the ground with our foreheads.

Attitude then is much more than mood—it is a method. Gaining a better attitude is simply positioning ourselves constructively in relation to our circumstances—and getting back to work—*no matter what mood we are in.* It is the most important factor in reaching our desired destination in life, in love, in marriage, in business—and in an airplane! It is what makes the difference between transcending the treetops, or slamming at full throttle into the jungle floor.

And after "shot happened" to me, I had quite a circumstance—especially for a young boy—to transcend.

At a fairly young age, as I began my speaking career, I coined the term "attitude therapy" to describe a method or process of training your brain to deal with tough situations. I had no idea how technically inaccurate I was in how I used the term "attitude," yet how dead on target I was in what maintaining a constructive position toward my circumstances would accomplish.

Author Charles Swindoll made an outstanding statement that has shifted the way we deal with tough circumstances. He said:

The longer I live, the more I realize the impact one's attitude has on life… we have a choice every day regarding the attitude we will embrace for that day…
I am convinced that life is ten percent what happens to me, and ninety percent how I react to it…

It is our attitude—our position—we take towards our circumstance that determines how we react (I prefer to say "respond") to it. That is the essence of what I used to call "Attitude Therapy." Now I call it common sense! (My kids call it "No, duh!")

Fellow speaker and author, Kate Adamson, in her book *Paralyzed but not Powerless,* suggests that when we are in trouble, rather than waste time thinking about what we don't want, we should focus on what we do want. And rather than think about what we can't do, focus on what we can do. Kate successfully dealt with total paralysis as a result of a double-pontine (brainstem) stroke by using this powerful, but oh-so-simple technique of *repositioning* herself mentally and getting to the hard work of physical rehabilitation.

As a keynote speaker, she now suggests that the key to success—especially when dealing with paralyzing difficulties—is to focus on what you have, desire, and can do—and let that guide your efforts. That is a great position, Kate.

Medical professionals are beginning to realize that your body will heal quicker if you take a positive or constructive position relative to your circumstances, regardless of your mood or the pain you are in. Feelings or moods are important. They strongly influence what we do, but it is our position that determines our moods and that is something we can consciously choose.

Sit in the physical position of Rodin's classic statue *The Thinker*, with your chin resting on your relaxed fist, and notice how you will tend to become thoughtful. Stand up with your jaw jutting out and notice how quickly you start to feel belligerent—even when there is nothing to be belligerent about.

Sometimes I ask my audience to try and shout "hurrah" from the position of Rodin's Thinker. They can hardly get it out. They are not in the right physical position. They are also not in the right mental or emotional position to be shouting enthusiastically. They are in the physical attitude of thoughtfulness, which has a huge effect on their emotional and mental attitude.

Cross your arms in a resistant position and notice how you start feeling resistant and close-minded. Go ahead, do it right now. Cross your arms in a defiant stance. Now, in that physical attitude, try to be open-minded about something. Notice how your physical position affects your mood. By taking a closed position we make it difficult to feel open-minded. The converse is also true. By adopting an open position, physically, our mental position becomes more open.

Stand or sit erect and see if you feel more alert and energetic. Slump and notice how you tend to become depressed or tired.

The late Earl Nightingale suggested that if we would act as if we were successful, we will become successful. Fellow speaker Brad Barton calls Nightingale the father of portable PMA because he popularized the idea of listening to positive messages while you are sitting in the car—stuck in traffic.

I prefer to say it like this: "Take the position—physically—that you are happy or energetic, thoughtful, compassionate, etc. and you will tend to *become* happy, energetic, thoughtful, and compassionate. The shift will happen fairly quickly—often in seconds. It may be dramatic or it may be subtle, but it will happen; and that shift creates an even more positive or constructive mental or emotional position.

The airplane conveying two hundred thirty passengers along the route known as Flight X was not in a bad mood. It was, however, in a bad or dangerous position—its "attitude" was wrong, especially when it was headed straight down at full throttle.

Intentional positive re-positioning—whether mental, spiritual, emotional, or financial—produces an upward spiral. Negative or destructive positioning produces a downward spiral that can end in disaster—just like Flight X.

CHAPTER 8

Onward and… Well, Onward

I received a lot of physical and occupational therapy following my accident and I am deeply grateful for it. Even so, the best therapy was the therapy I gave myself. As I said, back then I called it "Attitude Therapy." It was not about trying to change a situation; rather, it was about changing me—and how I responded to or otherwise dealt with situations. Regardless of how much help I received from those attending me, I knew intuitively that the greatest therapy was in my mind—and consisted of what I convinced myself to believe and to do and to become.

I knew that I would have physical limitations, but I also began to realize that within these limitations, somehow I could achieve anything I decided to achieve—even if I had to do it differently than what I had originally planned. From where I sat (pun intended), there was to be no holding back and I began to relish the challenge of each new day.

I made up my mind that I would overcome the hurdle of my paralysis and pain and find a different way to travel. I believed I could do anything; I would just do it differently.

Before I left the hospital, I was awarded the accolade, "Patient of the Month" for my positive attitude and influence on the staff and patients in the rehabilitation division. Nevertheless, my parents were again warned by the social workers that after going home and the reality of my life settled in, I would be very frustrated. They again warned my parents and me that I would go through screaming fits, periods of extreme depression and black moods. Why didn't that ever happen? I believe it is because I took responsibility for my situation and gave myself heavy doses of my newly coined "attitude therapy" every day. Sometimes it was memorizing a poem or a thought—or writing a poem or a thought. Other times it was closing my eyes and counting my blessings—focusing on what I had left, not what I had lost.

There is something else. At the risk of sounding too "preachy," let me tell you what a friend of mine does. He starts listing the things that are right with his life. His health, his friends (like me), his skills and talents, etc. He says he has never made it to the end of the list before he runs out of time and has to get back to work. During this exercise, his position shifts from what he has lost to what he has left. It worked for him, just as it worked for me.

Try it—right now. Start listing the things that you have or things about you that you appreciate. Notice how one thing reminds you of another and your "thank list" starts expanding exponentially. If you are willing to take a little time, see if you can ever get to the end of the list. You won't. It isn't a single stem that takes you in one direction until you reach the end; it is a genealogy tree that branches out to infinity. (I am from Utah. Genealogy is our specialty!) You start with a single benefit or blessing and that leads to others and on and on, branching out and out and out—each blessing or advantage or asset reminding you of another, and another, and yet another.

Choosing to focus on what you have left, rather than what you have lost when you are in a tough situation, is literally a mental position. It is a choice. Have you lost something? A job? A marriage? Your health? Precious possessions? What is your position with regard to your life? Are you cursed or blessed—are you both? Of course you are; but where do you want your focus to be? Turn to the left and look at your troubles and trials and trauma. Or turn to the right and look at your opportunities and assets. Don't force it. Just try it—once a day. Once a day take the position of looking to the right, so to speak, and once in a while see if you can possibly run out of good things before you run out of time.

Then watch how this "positive positioning" changes how you feel and increases your personal energy. Notice too that it is your change of position that changes your mood, not the other way around!

Sometimes my positive positioning meant taking a different position towards my changing body. I started gaining muscle on the top while my legs atrophied. I accepted that even though my lower body would atrophy, I could still love myself from the inside out. (Besides, my upper body was getting really buff—and the girls noticed!)

Think about it this way. The average person spends forty-five minutes every day looking good for the world on the outside. We comb, shave, put on makeup (well, I don't usually put on makeup, unless my speech is being televised) and we spend a lot of time doing it. Why not spend just as much time "looking good" on the inside by giving ourselves a forty-five minute dose of positive positioning each day?

Harvard Medical School each year holds a conference called Spirituality in Healing. Attendees learn that the mind, body, and spirit are very much connected. With or without me and this book, you can "train the brain" how to think and respond more constructively towards your circumstances. Hopefully, this book will help you do that more effectively. Look at your own situations with the position that no matter what happens, you will still accomplish your dreams, even if you have to do it somewhat differently that you originally planned.

You can't just tell someone to have a good attitude and *shazaam,* they instantly change like magic. It takes time and a lot of counseling or self-talk—or both. In fact, I used to say the same thing myself—but it isn't true. You can have a good attitude instantly—as long as you remember that "attitude" isn't "mood"; it is "position." It is possible to simply decide to take a different position—and do it. Furthermore, it is possible to do it *immediately*. Now it isn't always easy, especially at first; it's a skill that has to be learned and developed. But it is simple—and with time and practice it becomes natural, spontaneous and eventually it can become easy, just like any physical or mental skill you practice.

As Ralph Waldo Emerson once said, "That which we persist in doing becomes easier for us to do; not that the nature of the thing itself is changed, but that our power to do is increased."

As I have said, when I was first injured, humor was an important coping mechanism. As my lower body atrophied—something that was pretty hard for this former all-star quarterback to take—I had to practice and exercise that sense of humor. I would say things like, "Jeepers! My legs look like I went on a diet from the waist down."

We are really like computers. What we put into our minds and spirits and hearts is what comes out. As we used to say in the 1960s when computers began to find their place in our world, "garbage in—garbage out." We must put positive in before positive can come out.

I make this sound so easy. It isn't. It is simple, but it is not always, or even usually, "easy." My accident didn't push me completely over the edge. However, there were times I would have very much liked to close my eyes and not wake up. I did notice that, while the circumstances didn't change, I did. One of my favorite sayings is: "So often we seek for a change in our circumstances, when all we really need to do is change our position."

For some time—occasionally it still happens—I would go to sleep and dream of running and playing with my friends or my big brother. Then I'd wake up with a wheelchair sitting next to my bed, disappointed to find myself still paralyzed, aching from top to bottom, sparking pain—electrical shocks firing randomly from my damaged central nervous system like a shorted out robot—and nothing but the upper half of my torso working. Sometimes I would lie there and wish it was all over—or it had never happened.

Well, I did what anyone would do, and does do, when dealing with a major loss. But, as I became fully awake, I continued my habit of looking at what did work—not what didn't—and thanking my God for what I had left, and essentially ignoring what I had lost. Life moved inexorably up and up. Life is pretty great today.

I was always a goal setter before my accident. I thought of my future and visualized doing great things like playing college basketball or being the high school student body president and quarterback or team captain—and those things tended to happen.

Following my accident, I did the same thing. I wasn't sure what the next day would bring. But really, had I ever? I felt that overall things would work out and positive things would happen as they always had. It had been my habit of thinking and it continued to be my habit of thinking, only this time it wasn't an unconscious habit—it was now a skill, consciously and intentionally nurtured and practiced.

If I dealt constructively with the present, a positive future would naturally result. I couldn't go back to school until I could get dressed. I couldn't drive a car until I could transfer myself into the car. I couldn't get a girl to like me unless I liked myself. So, I learned to dress myself, transfer to my car—and like myself. Fortunately, the last one was the easiest, because I am such a dang nice guy.

I had to learn to dress myself and transfer safely. (If I can't transfer I can't drive. If I can't drive, I can't get girls. If I can't get girls, why live, right?) Learning to dress myself or drive with hand controls may not seem like a big deal to some people; however, each of these small successes was essential to the reaching of my great big dreams. Even though as a child, I had already learned to dress myself, I now had to re-learn how to do it—but do it differently. Thanks to the attitudes instilled in me by my parents and coaches, though, it didn't really slow me down. Like jumping over a ditch, I just had to step back before I could jump forward.

My goals, therefore, became simple things like learning to transfer effectively from bed to chair without bouncing off the floor, and moving from chair to vehicle with some semblance of grace and dignity.

There were some things that were a bit more difficult and complicated. For example, curbs were formidable barriers. I had to learn to pop a wheelie and jump the curb because the wheels can't gain traction on the corner of the curb, especially if it is painted. Before my accident, I never thought twice about stepping up on a curb, but when you are in a wheelchair, a six-inch rounded and painted curb (painted curbs are really slick) is a significant obstacle.

As I mentioned, the principles in this book actually began to form while I was still in the hospital. I thought about my new situation as a challenge to overcome—an obstacle, a goal—just as in any athletic event. Life gave me a new game to play—and win.

Looking back, this thing I named "Attitude Therapy" didn't stop me from having bad days, but it kept me from having bad weeks and months—and clearly kept me from having a bad life. Some think fourteen-year-old kids don't think too deeply, but when challenging circumstances arise, we will think just as deeply as we need to in order to rise above our circumstances.

When I returned home from the hospital, I expected some serious sympathy. I didn't get it. What I didn't know was that my parents had discussed my situation at length, and had determined to treat me no differently than they had before. That was part of their evil plan to help me deal with life by taking the position that I was a normal contributing member of society—the same position I was in before the shooting. With the inspiration and support of my wonderful parents, family, and friends, I adopted this position too, and it has served me well—but at first, it wasn't much fun.

I had as many chores as anyone else. I worked just as hard as they did, but I did it differently. My parents made it clear that my contribution was still needed in order for the family to succeed. I had always been an important part of my dad's crew—and he made it clear that I still was. We were a big family with a big house and a big lawn, garden and orchard—and it took a big family to run it. I had to do my part— and it was obvious that my part was just as important as anyone else's. Someone had to sort fruit; someone had to fix sprinkler heads; someone had to do dishes and clean the bathroom. As in any corporation's "reasonable accommodation" effort, my duties were shifted to fit what I was more capable of doing. I became a qualified domestic—without a French maid's apron or English butler's waistcoat.

Just as in corporate disability accommodation, sometimes the reassignment didn't work. Initially, I was assigned to "garden duty." I had to wheel myself along between the rows of vegetables, and lean over to weed by hand. The leaning over taught me some important things about balance (actually it was the "falling over" that taught me about balance) and I still use those skills today; but wheeling through the soft earth was a different thing. It was awkward and extremely difficult. I came in exhausted, dirty and muddy. I was to learn later that Mom often watched me and wept from behind the kitchen curtains. But she and Dad had agreed that I needed the experience and the exercise and she held firm until it became obvious that I was destroying more carrots than I was cultivating. Messing up the carpeting when I came in with mud all over the wheels was the last straw, and I was finally relieved of this "reassignment" and *re*-reassigned another chore until my "job description" fit me—rather than the other way around.

Extremely flexible in accommodating my disability, my folks let me figure out the "how" of my duties. They supplied the "what" and there was really not much discussion afterward—they let me figure it out myself, which is what I wanted. Their firm though flexible approach to my disablement helped immensely in my seeing myself as "normal." Their lack of "micro-management" helped me learn to cope with my responsibilities—to learn in my own way, to do things that my siblings did—even though I had to do them differently.

In the long run, I was a much better person for the way I was managed by my parents. As they got used to my condition, they got better at assigning things for me to do that were more suitable to my condition. They helped me believe that, aside from murdering baby carrots in the garden, there wasn't anything I couldn't do.

Sometimes I did feel like I was a burden. Sometimes I still do. I had to be carried up and down stairs—and we had to knock out a wall on the main level and create a bedroom and bathroom for me—but no one ever said I was a burden or even an inconvenience (I chose to believe them—most of the time). They seemed to think that I was worth the extra effort—and I have spent the rest of my life proving that they were right.

CHAPTER 9

The Perils of Paralysis

S oon after the shooting, I learned that even though I couldn't feel anything from my chest down, my body wasn't dead. *It* could feel. I just didn't know it. Once I transferred into the bathtub and turned on the warm water—at least I thought it was warm. It was actually very *hot*. When the hot water hit my foot, my foot wasn't pleased and my leg tried to help it get out of the water by jerking spasmodically and flinging it about like a disjointed marionette. I stared at it for a second, shocked, while I tried to figure out what was going on. Steam was the clue. I quickly turned off the hot water but it was too late. I paid for my mistake with a blistered foot that took months to heal.

I can't feel it when I get injured. Furthermore, the paralyzed part of my body doesn't heal well. From the chest down the circulation is reduced because my muscles are slack. Trust me on this: cardiovascular exercise is very important for people of all ages. The action of muscles "massaging" the veins helps return the blood to the heart. Once those muscles cease to function, circulation becomes more sluggish.

I have to be aware of any cuts or abrasions—or burns. Every night I feel my buttocks and check them out in a mirror. My wife thinks I'm vain; but actually, I'm checking for decubitus sores (bedsores). Bedsores can be a major problem. If I get them, I go back to the hospital and lie on my stomach for a month while they heal. Sometimes having such sores requires surgery. In reality, sitting on my butt too long can be dangerous and expensive.

Life is filled with peril when you can't feel pain. One hot summer afternoon, I was riding with my friend Roger Dayton in his old green pickup truck. The metal floorboards always got very hot in the summer. I was barefoot and since I had no feeling in my feet, I didn't know how hot the floor was until I began smelling barbecued meat. What I didn't realize was that *I* was the barbecue! The soles of my feet were cooked almost to the bone. The only good thing about this was that I had no pain—of course, that was also the problem.

A few years ago, I shattered my lower left leg and ankle snowmobiling. I didn't feel a thing. I didn't know I had broken my leg—in sixteen places—until we got back to the cabin and were taking off my boots and my lower leg flopped sideways in a way God never intended. I wore a cast for three months. I still walk with a limp—*I wish.*

The perils of paralysis are many. The whole world is taller than I am. Shot happens and then "short happens." I can't adjust hotel shower heads or reach things on upper store shelves. I can only buy children's cereal and toys because they stock store shelves according to age appeal (good thing I am easily entertained). It is the same at home—except my family understands "reasonable accommodation" just as good corporations do. Cups and glasses are in the bottom drawer so I can reach them. You get the point.

I apologized to my wife once about not being able to change a light bulb. She smiled sweetly, kissed me on top of my head (which really helped my masculine ego) and said "Honey, I would rather have someone like you who *can't* change a light bulb than someone who *won't.*

A friend of mine remodeled his house to accommodate his disability. He lowered his whole kitchen—sinks, counters, cabinets—he did the same in the bathrooms and everywhere. He says he took his house to a tailor and had it altered to fit. I love his house, but I can't do that to mine. I have a family. As much as I'd like to, I can't change the world to fit my disability. I have to live in a world of inconvenience or I would be inconveniencing. Frankly, I don't want a counter adjusted for me, because then I'd have to do the dishes.

By the way, there are some accommodations that have been made in my home that benefit others too. For example, my little kids like having the cups in the lower drawers. They also enjoy toy car and roller blade races down my wheelchair ramp in the garage.

The world benefits from these accommodations just as my family does. Delivery drivers love ramps in stores and businesses—so do folks with babies in strollers. Most everyone likes automatic door push plates, wider aisles, and larger bathroom stalls, all of which were created for those of us in wheelchairs. There should be tickets issued for able-bodies who use those wide bathroom stalls, as there are tickets issued for using the handicap parking stalls without special plates or tags—except I don't know who would be on potty patrol (maybe police officers on disciplinary status).

Even with these growing accommodations in the workplace and the marketplace, I learned early that I have to meet the world *more* than halfway. My family wasn't about to play with the paddleboats in the city park duck pond instead of motorboating in wild and remote Lake Powell. They would just pack me up, toss me in back of the Suburban and take off (The only time I have any dignity is when I drive). It was the best thing they could have done. They treated me as though I was normal (normal luggage) and took me along wherever they went.

Once in a while I might take advantage of a special program or activity for the disabled. But as the years went by, I realized that many of those activities are difficult for my family to take part in.

My family treated me as a normal person within reasonable parameters and made reasonable demands with reasonable accommodation, so I was reasonably willing to do most everything they did—within reason.

I appreciate disability accommodation. I love the enhanced sensitivity of this wonderful country towards those of us who deal with disabilities. I love it when cities set aside certain parking spaces for the disabled and when companies build ramps to help us get around better.

I also feel that I need to return the favor and reasonably accommodate the realities of life. You can build a ramp where I can move physically to a higher elevation, but I have to build my own mental ramp to elevate my attitude above my circumstances. You see, no matter how much accommodation I am given, there are some things I have to do on my own. There isn't always someone around to help me get back in my chair after flipping over backwards or pitching over sideways on a slippery slope. I have learned how to set my chair up and "remount" by myself, not an easy thing to do at my level of disability.

From a sitting position, I have to set upright my tipped-over chair, scoot over close to it, and lift my dead weight a height of twenty-four inches with arms that are only six inches longer than my torso. With one hand on the ground and another on the chair, I pull with my right and push with my left. Let's see you try it. No cheating, now. You can't use any muscles from your chest down.

Whenever I am in a serious bind, I bless the name of Dr. Martin Cooper. Who is Martin Cooper? He's the inventor of cell phones. (Or was it Al Gore? Al claims to have invented the Internet. Maybe he also thinks he invented cell phones—and fire.)

CHAPTER 10

Don't be a Knee-Jerk Jerk

I turned sixteen a little over a year after the shooting. A family rite of passage—a family tradition that was very important to me—occurred on my sixteenth birthday. It was to go deer hunting with the entire family. It was a big deal, a huge family affair involving my parents, my brothers, my grandparents, cousins, uncles, aunts, etc.

Even though I would not be able to stomp through the trees and brush, and would be hunting from a sitting position, I was included—and I was excited.

The opening morning of deer hunting season finally arrived. Before I knew it, I was sitting behind my dad on my grandfather's chestnut quarter horse. My paralyzed legs were wrapped around Dad's waist with my shoelaces tied together in front of him to hold me in place (sometimes I'm luggage, sometimes I'm a backpack). Even in that ignoble position, I still loved the ride through the golden fall leaves of the quaking aspen as we moved down into the valleys of the beautiful Pahvant Mountain Range, east of Fillmore, Utah.

We finally decided on a good spot for me to position myself. They lifted me off the horse, propped me up against an old aspen, handed me my Uncle's .30-30 Winchester lever action rifle (just like John Wayne's), tossed me a sack lunch, and walked off saying they'd be back at noon.

They went down into the canyon below me to hunt—and perhaps scare some deer up my way. Soon, I could hear the animals rustle through the dry leaves as they moved towards me. As I waited quietly under the tree with my sack lunch beside me, I realized that what was coming toward me could be anything: squirrels, porcupine, deer, elk, bear, cougar, Bengal tigers, Big Foot. Suddenly I realized *I* could be lunch.

I had not been there long when a herd of a dozen or so elk came along, paying me no mind whatsoever. I watched them, enthralled with their beauty and majesty. I was also nervous. I felt extremely vulnerable. I couldn't move. I could imagine them trampling me into the ground. I had no way to save myself. I didn't even think about the gun. It wasn't elk season and I didn't want to go to jail—getting trampled to death, notwithstanding.

After they moved on, I heard other noises. Probably deer over the ridge, but in my mind I could still see a big hungry bear coming toward me with me on his menu and the apple in my sack lunch for dessert.

Instead, after a paranoia-filled wait, a nice two-point buck came into the clearing about fifty yards below. My heart pounded as I swung my rifle to my shoulder, aimed carefully, took a deep breath, let it half out, and squeezed the trigger. I had a peep sight, not a scope, but I dropped him with one shot.

It was a nice first-time trophy. I couldn't have been more proud. After years of hunting with my dad and carrying our lunches in my backpack, I had come of age. I had finally bagged my own deer.

Suddenly, the deer jumped up—or tried to. I hadn't killed him. My bullet had simply broken his back—just as my friend's bullet had done to me. The young buck began dragging himself along with his front legs, trying to escape. I couldn't get a clear shot to end his pain. I watched helplessly, sick to my stomach. Suddenly there was a loud explosion off to my left. A passing hunter had seen the situation and ended the paralyzed animal's life.

He walked over to me wondering why I was just sitting there under the tree. I explained my situation and what had happened. He offered to field-dress the deer and I gladly accepted. Before I knew it, he had dragged the deer to a nearby tree, cleaned and dressed it, left it hanging to cool, and was on his way.

When my dad and the others returned for lunch, they were startled to see that not only had I killed my first deer, but imagine their surprise to see it hanging in a tree, field-dressed and ready to carry out.

When I first realized the deer had been paralyzed by my bullet, I had a surge of empathy and sadness. My deer was no different than me. I knew its pain, sense of despair, the broken back, the loss of freedom and mobility.

The increase of meat for our family's table was important, and I did love the trek to the mountains, but even though I still enjoy the adventure, I never looked at hunting quite the same way.

The next summer, I went with my family and my friend, Roger Dayton, to Deer Creek Reservoir for a day of water-skiing. I was confined to the boat. I hadn't yet learned to water-ski, but I had learned to have fun.

After all the others had finished skiing, they decided it was Mike's turn. All we had was a round yellow plywood board that Roger had brought along. They tied a long nylon rope to the board and tossed it into the water behind the boat. They had invented a new water sport: "Drag Mikey!"

I was up for it, so I buckled on my bright orange life jacket, transferred to the edge of the boat and, like Humpty Dumpty, tipped over into the frigid water. It was the strangest sensation. The only part of my body that actually felt cold was the non-paralyzed part above where I had been shot. The lower part of my body (from the bullet scar down) felt nothing. Actually, it seemed kinda' warm by comparison—as though I was wearing a wetsuit.

Treading water with my dead legs dangling beneath me, I felt like fish bait for Jaws. I pulled myself onto this makeshift ski, grabbed hold of the thick nylon rope, and signaled for my dad to open the throttle.

We took off at full speed and I found myself hanging on for dear life on an improvised boogie-board (there were no special water skis for the disabled). This was less like skiing and more like being dragged to death in a Roman arena.

Cold spray hit me hard in the face. I became disoriented and a little scared. *This isn't very much fun. Why did my friend shoot me? I am having a bad day.*

Even though the water was hitting me in the face, I could still see that everyone in our boat was watching me and laughing. I thought maybe one of my sisters, Julie or Collette, had told a joke. But then I remembered that neither of them was funny. Maybe they were laughing at my paralyzed legs flapping behind me. I didn't know what was going on, but I didn't like them laughing at me especially when I already felt awkward and very uncomfortable.

I looked over my shoulder and saw that my atrophied legs were indeed flapping in the breeze like a flying frog. I looked towards the shore and was certain the picnickers and sunbathers were all pointing and staring at me. I was giving everyone a good laugh. It seemed pretty insensitive to me.

Then I found out what everyone was really laughing about. To my horror, I realized that the jet of water coming from underneath the board had ripped off my sporty lime green swimming trucks. I had become the world's first nude disabled water skier.

Embarrassed, I quickly let go of the rope slid off the board and waited for Dad to circle around in the boat and pick me up. Bobbing up and down in freezing cold water, I thought, "It isn't my fault that I am up to my neck in freezing cold water. It isn't my fault I lost my swimming trunks. It isn't my fault I got shot. *This isn't very much fun. Why did my friend shoot me? I'm having a bad day.*

I was angry and humiliated and looking for someone to blame. I *needed* someone to blame. Otherwise, I would have to take responsibility for this—and, as I said, it wasn't my fault.

Though I was mortified and angry at first, I guess the frigid water cooled me off and I began to think. Moments ticked by as I waited for the boat to return. I realized that this moment was a microcosm of my accident and how it affected my life. I couldn't change what had happened, but I could change how I responded to it.

Somewhere in the process of learning to deal with the tough circumstances of my young life, I learned three important words, "take personal responsibility." Or is that *four* words: Take–Personal–Response–Ability.

Please understand the difference between "responsibility" and "fault." It wasn't necessarily my fault I got shot, but it was (and still is) my responsibility to deal with the consequences and the circumstances created by that unfortunate event.

You see, regardless of fault or blame, we have the ability to respond to whatever circumstances or situations we find ourselves in. We can't always choose what happens to us, nor are we really in control of our immediate emotional or physical *reactions*, but we do retain the most important choice: how we *respond*.

> *Between stimulus and response there is a space. In that*
> *space is our power to choose our response. In our response*
> *lies our growth and our freedom.*
> —Viktor E. Frankl, "Man's Search for Meaning"

Our ability to choose how (or even if) we will respond to a situation or circumstance may be the main thing that sets us apart from the beasts.

I am not suggesting that we shouldn't have feelings or reactions. That is a natural part of the human condition. I am also not suggesting that we bury those feelings. I am suggesting that we can do something to minimize our immediate reactions—if they are negative or destructive—by transforming them into positive constructive reactions.

How do we do that? How do we turn our immediate, knee-jerk, negative reactions into positive reactions? (After all, we don't want to be a knee-jerk jerk!) We start with our attitude—our position. What emotional, physical or mental position would we like to take relative to the situation or potential situation? We decide ahead of time what our position will be regarding that situation. *Then* we decide what *response* we feel would be most appropriate under those or similar circumstances. *Then* we practice that conscious response until it becomes an unconscious reflex.

Aren't we then still reacting? Yes, we are. That is what a reaction is, a quick, automatic, habitual response. The difference, however, is that now our reaction is positive and constructive. We are reacting the way we have *chosen* to react. Our position towards this kind of situation provides the framework for creating a thoughtful, disciplined, and constructive response. We then practice that predetermined response until it becomes a positive reflex—a positive *reaction* that replaces the old negative reaction.

How do we practice prior to the event? Just like any trained athlete. My teammate whips me the ball from out-of-bounds. I fake a shot at the basket—it actually would be a fairly good shot so the defensive player takes the bait and goes into the air. I bounce-pass to my teammate who is wide open under the hoop, and he scores the winning basket.

How do I discipline my reflexes so I would sacrifice a good shot in a good situation and pass off to a teammate in a better position for a better shot—and give my team the championship? How do I change an undisciplined reaction to take a good shot into a disciplined reaction to pass to someone who has a better shot? How do you take an undisciplined negative reaction to a curt store clerk, a petulant child, an angry spouse—and turn it into a disciplined positive response? Practice, practice, and more practice.

Begin with your attitude—a position you decide you want to take toward a situation that might ordinarily throw you off your game. Decide what action would be consistent with that position, and then practice mentally and physically until the undisciplined negative reaction gives way to a disciplined positive reaction. Practice makes perfect? Perhaps not, but practice does make positive and productive.

> *Understanding the nature of the problem is halfway to the solution.*
> —A. Einstein (German/American physicist)

> *Taking the appropriate position relative to the problem is the other half of the solution.*
> —M. Schlappi (German/American wheelchair athlete)

Einstein was a pretty smart fellow. He knew that ignoring problems was no way to solve them. He knew that understanding the problem was an essential part of the solution; but, more than that, he understood the importance of understanding the *nature* of the problem as the first essential step of solving the problem.

What is the difference between understanding the problem and understanding the *nature* of the problem? Simply understanding the problem is primarily a determination of the facts. However, understanding the *nature* of the problem is much more. It is understanding the genesis of the problem. What created it? What and who are affected by it? And what the dynamics of it are?

Einstein knew that the more time one spent constructively analyzing the situation to determine the nature of the difficulty or problem, the closer one would be to discovering or determining a valid solution. Getting clear about what the situation is—what happened, when, what and whom it affects and how—is the nature of the problem. That provides the keys to the solution.

In my case, understanding the problem is simple. I got shot. A .38 caliber bullet pierced my chest and lodged in my spine. I was paralyzed from the chest down. I am still paralyzed. Those are the facts. *That* is the problem.

The *nature* of the problem is a bit more involved. I can't do jump shots or drive without hand controls. My best friend shot me. My girlfriend left me. It altered the course of my life in ways that few can even comprehend.

There is more. How was my friend Torrey impacted? How was his family impacted? How was *my* family impacted? How was the community affected? How about my football team, my girlfriend, and every other relationship I had and every relationship I ever will have? What and who caused the situation. What and who is impacted. That is the nature of the problem. That is what I had to deal with, and still have to deal with if I am to continue to deal effectively with my disability.

What about you? What's your problem? What have you been hit with? Is there something lodged in your heart or soul that paralyzes you? What are the simple facts? That is the problem.

Now, what is the *nature* of the problem? What happened? Why did it happen? How does your situation affect you? Your family? Your friendships? Your team? Your career? Your life? That is the nature of the problem.

Once you analyze and understand the nature of your problem, you are halfway to your solution. (You ought to know where you are on the court before you take the shot, right?)

The second half is deciding what position you will take relative to your problem—now that you understand what the nature of the problem really is. That position or attitude will determine whether the problem—or you—will control your life.

What are you going to do about your problem, regardless of whose fault it is? In saying "whose fault," I really mean who or what, through action or inaction, caused or allowed harm to come to you? Will this thing change the course of your life? Will you take the position that everything will work out and move ahead, achieving everything you intended to achieve anyway?

Did my paralysis really alter—in a negative way—the ultimate or intended course or the meaning or results of my life? I doubt it. If I hadn't been shot, I may have become a great professional basketball player. I may have leapt into the air, made great three point shots, and then traveled about the world, entertaining and inspiring thousands with stories of my victories.

But I was shot and, instead of becoming a professional basketball player, I became an amateur (Olympic!) basketball player, sitting on my butt and making great three point shots from my wheelchair. And in spite of the chair, I have traveled about the world, inspiring thousands with my story (perhaps hundreds of thousands if enough people buy this book!).

In taking a position relative to a situation, we accept personal responsibility—but in a way that's different than what is commonly perceived in our society and culture.

"Responsibility" simply means the *ability* to *respond*. It has nothing to do with being at fault or liable. The proof of the meaning of the word lies in its root structure: respons-ibility, then, is "response-ability."

For example, when I say that I accept responsibility, I don't mean that I take the *blame*. The *ability* to *respond* has nothing to do with fault or blame. If I accept responsibility for a given situation, it doesn't necessarily imply that I had anything to do with causing it. It simply means I accept that I can respond to the situation regardless of who or what caused it. My ability to respond is a separate issue and really the only relevant one. Who or what caused the situation is already in the past, so fault or blame, while relevant perhaps to a judge or an insurance assessor, is irrelevant to me.

Do I accept responsibility for what happens to me? Yes, of course. What about what happens to you? Do I accept responsibility for *that?* If you're thinking that I just asked you a trick question, you're right.

As a speaker and writer, I do accept "response-ability" for what has happened to you. Does that mean I caused it? No. It just means that I will respond to it by helping *you* deal with it. That is why I wrote this book.

What if I truly don't understand how to respond to my wife when she's upset? Well, listening is a response—often the best response. Sometimes, it's the *only* response I can offer and, more often than not, it is the *safest* response.

And what about you? Are you "response-able" for my situation? Your neighbor's? Your co-workers? Your employees? The ancient Egyptians? Are you able to respond regardless of what happened or who or what was the cause? Yes. Even by ignoring the situation, or deciding you can or will do nothing about it, you are responding to it.

Accept that you have the ability to respond. Then take the high road and respond with your highest ability, regardless of whose "fault" the circumstances might be.

Immediately following the shooting, I took responsibility for it. I accepted my ability to respond to it. I determined to deal with the situation constructively. I continued that attitude through rehab. I made it a habit to respond constructively to whatever happened. That was and is my position. I could lay blame at the feet of my friend who shot me. But what would it gain me?

I am not telling you that it would be wrong to determine fault or blame. I am only suggesting that to do so, even if justified, simply regurgitates the event. Whether the cause of a harmful situation is a sentient being or an act of fate or nature, blame is for the courts or God to deal with; but for me, repeating the identification of the fault or blame does no constructive good. It is a waste of good energy or resources that would likely better serve me in moving forward, rather than looking back.

I have a bullet lodged in my spine. My friend put it there. The bullet's impact paralyzed me. I am still paralyzed. It has dramatically affected my life, my work—my life's work—my relationships. It still does. It probably always will. Oh well.

Now that I have identified the nature of the problem, what will I do about it? How will I respond to it? I will move forward.

This is not self-restraint or self-control. This is conditioning—intentionally replacing knee-jerk reactions that tend to create problems for us with new, more positive and constructive responses. How? Practice! Practice, practice, and more practice.

A friend of mine, a relationship coach, said that one of his college professors used to invite his students to say derogatory things to him just to see if they could catch him off guard and get a negative reaction from him. They never could. Why? He wasn't "on guard." He was practiced. He had conditioned himself to react in a constructive way in exactly the same way an athlete conditions him or herself to react constructively in a tense or pressured situation.

By reacting to his student's creative insults with his constructive (and often funny) reactions, he proved we need not get offended and reactive ("emotionally hijacked," he called it) just because someone is trying to push our buttons—*or we think they are.* My friend told of a fellow student trying to insult the professor by telling him that his pants were ugly and outdated. The professor smiled and thanked him for caring about how he looked.

The student was being rude, right? Well, maybe not. Perhaps he was really trying to be helpful. Maybe he liked this professor and wanted him to be in style like the rest of the "cool" guys. He just didn't say it right. Or maybe he *was* just being rude; after all, the professor had asked all of his students to surprise him from time to time with insults so he could practice his ability to react positively where he might ordinarily react negatively.

This professor demonstrated daily that we can react constructively in even negative situations by taking the position that we will always choose the best possible interpretation of intent when someone seems to be trying to "push our buttons." That is the foundation from which the positive response will be determined and, through practice, the positive reaction, established.

What pushes your buttons? A whining child? A nagging spouse? A demanding ex-spouse? A bossy boss? A snoopy neighbor? A rude driver, customer, supplier, etc? Do you react? Of course you do. The question is, will your reaction be constructive or destructive? That is up to you—ultimately, if not immediately.

If your initial reaction isn't constructive, let's see how to change that. First, notice how you react and think about why you react that way. Really analyze it. Be honest, but also be kind to yourself. There's a good reason why you feel the way you do and why you react the way you do.

"Why do you react the way you do? Is it the way you were taught?" Maybe you haven't even thought about it. Maybe it is simply the way you have always acted and no one has ever called you on it.

Also think about why the other party might be doing what he or she is doing. Examine others' actions with the same gentleness you would examine your own behavior. There are good reasons for their behavior, even if they aren't readily apparent. Those reasons are probably similar to the reasons we do inappropriate things even when we "know better."

If someone cuts you off in traffic, your initial reaction might be to say, "Why would he do that?" That's a good question. Ask yourself the question again. Why *would* he do that?

Now, take a moment and carefully think about the answer to that question. Why *would* a perfect stranger cut you off on the freeway just to get to an off-ramp? Why didn't he slow down and pull in behind you instead of whipping across three lanes of freeway traffic, cutting in front of you, taking your front bumper off and nearly killing twenty people in the process?

That *is* a good question. Now take another moment and answer it. "I don't know" is a pretty good answer. It's the truth. You *don't* know. Why *would* a perfect stranger want to offend you or endanger your life? He doesn't even know you. He wouldn't have a motive to offend you or hurt you. Maybe he wasn't trying to murder you. Mayhem might not be his motive.

But why would he drive like a maniac? I am glad you keep asking the question instead of assuming the answer. Maybe he is rushing to the hospital. Maybe his wife is pregnant. Maybe he is on his way back from a four week business trip and wants to get his wife pregnant! Or maybe he is a maniac—insane—deranged. The fact is we don't know why he is driving like that. There is a reason—maybe even a good reason—but we don't know what it is *and probably never will.*

So let's forget about what's going on in his mind, and let's think about what's going on in our minds. Let's also think about how we would *like* to respond to this situation—and to that driver and, after some practice, to similar situations in the future.

You see, *everyone* deserves reasonable accommodation from time to time, not just us guys in wheelchairs. Everyone deserves accommodation for their imperfections and disabilities. Sometimes worries, stresses, disturbances at home, business challenges, etc., create temporary insanity that causes us to erupt vocally—sometimes physically—and do stupid things that we ordinarily wouldn't do.

What do we do about the fellow who cuts us off on the freeway? We have a couple of choices. We can take the position that he is a jerk and is trying to kill us and we are justified in getting mad and chasing after him like a maniac so we can shake our fist at him. Or we can take the position that there is a good reason he is driving recklessly. He might need some understanding. Maybe he needs help. Maybe we should be empathetic. Maybe even offer a quick prayer to help keep him from hurting himself or someone else (Don't close your eyes during this prayer).

Which choice is easier on your blood pressure? To be angry or empathetic? Resolving to be more understanding and empathetic is perfectly rational and noble and it doesn't make you less of a man (or woman) to take the high road, move on up the highway toward your destination and let him continue on down the off ramp.

Once you realize that being forgiving and understanding feels good, and once you resolve to be a calm, rational adult, it is much easier to decide how you will respond to situations like this. "As a man thinketh, so is he," said the great James Allen, reflecting the wisdom of great men who had gone before him. I like to say it a little differently. It isn't just what we think, but what we do that makes us who we are. So perhaps it could be said, "As we react, so are we."

Someone once said (I think it was me) that great things can be accomplished by those who know *how*, but even greater things will be accomplished by those who know why—*and are resolved to make the change*. My editor wrote a funny poem about that kind of resolve. With his permission, I share it with you.

An Outlaw's Resolve

He finally resolved
To stop living a life of crime.
But was his decision soon enough?
Did he repent in time?
    It shouldn't matter, brother,
    because deep within his heart
    was an outlaw's sincere desire
    to make a bran' new start!
        As he sat astride his horse one morn,
        watchin' the rising sun,
        he said, "I *can* change my ways, by durn.
        I'll be as good as anyone!"
            "I *will* be a better man," he said,
            "I will completely change m' life.
            I'll settle down and have some kids.
            Mebbe even get me a wife!"
                He smiled in his resolve
                and said, "I *will* change, by heck!

I'll turn my life clean around
if they'll jes' get this rope
from off m' neck!"
© 2005 Tom Cantrell

What behavioral changes are you resolved to make? What pain in the neck do you want to avoid? Perhaps pain isn't what is motivating you to change. Perhaps you just want a better life—better results for you and your family or coworkers or supervisor or your employees—than you now enjoy.

Maybe you are already pretty good at the situation you are facing but you want to be better. You are a good parent, but you could be better. You are a good boss, but you could be better. You are a good athlete, but you could be better. When should you change? Maybe now?

Back to the lake. Here I am, treading water, with absentee swim shorts, waiting for Dad to circle the boat around and pluck me from the freezing water before Jaws could get me.

I am embarrassed. Having a "bad butt day" is much worse than having a "bad hair day." Now what do I do? I can sulk and get upset with how the others were acting, or I could appreciate the humor of the moment. Maybe I could even learn something from this.

As the boat came full circle, my attitude came full circle. I regained my composure (and what was left of my dignity) and resolved to take a different position about what had just happened.

Losing my shorts and my dignity created a tough moment. But the next moment was a gift. Though I had reacted in humiliation and anger, *no one saw it*. I was forced to wait—while the cold water cooled me off. That time of reflection—that cooling off period—was the gift. As the boat circled around to pick me up, I had time to choose a different response. I had lost my shorts but gained a new approach to tough situations.

My sister Julie tossed me her pullover shorts that matched her frilly florescent pink swim suit. I ducked under the water, and after a few tries, I managed to pull them on. Amid gales of laughter, my family dragged me back into the boat. I accepted the humor of the situation and the rest of the day was good.

CHAPTER 11

Cheer Up—Things Could Be Worse

Well, I cheered up, and sure enough—things got worse!

Several months after the shooting accident, I found myself arm-wrestling with Coach Fuller, my weight-lifting coach. We were in his social studies classroom, and my new girlfriend was watching. I had to win.

Like bull elephants competing for dominance, we went all out. It was the unstoppable force meeting the immovable object. Something had to give. It did. My arm gave. There was a loud pop and searing agony as my funny bone ripped free of my elbow and shoved its way into my wrist.

Coach won the contest, breaking my arm in the process, and leaving me racked with pain. My funny bone was broken—and it wasn't funny. I spent the next ninety days covered in a blue fiberglass cast that extended from the palm of my hand to my shoulder.

Not only was this injury painful, it greatly limited my ability to get around. Before the contest, I was a paraplegic with two good arms to propel myself along. Now I was a tri-plegic! I went "in circles" for the next three months—getting nowhere. This interruption in my progress, though, was a blessing in a way. It caused me to learn entirely new dimensions of patience. It also taught me a lesson. I showed off, was stubborn, and got what I had coming.

I also got the lead out—literally. While I was under sedation getting my broken arm set, the doctor flipped me over and surgically removed the bullet from my back. Prior to this, it had felt like an extra vertebra in my spine.

After waking, I held this little chunk of lead in the palm of my hand and thought about all the pain and damage it had caused. Something came to me in that moment. I discovered that holding something and hanging onto something are not the same things. I held the bullet in my hand and at the same time, let it go.

Sadly, my friend did not let it go. We stayed friends for a year or so before Torrey's family moved away. We'd go to movies and parties and hang out at the mall. In fact, people who did not know about my situation would see us together, with me in a wheelchair, and ask me what happened. I would gesture toward Torrey and wryly state, "He shot me." They would chuckle, not fully understanding the joke, and move on.

I still have that bullet. It is hung on a ribbon like my other medals. I have two gold, two bronze, and a lead. Which do you think is the most significant? Getting the lead out of my back and out of my heart and mind was more rewarding and empowering than the medals I eventually won with my team. In fact "getting the lead out" was what brought me to so many personal and team victories.

Shot happens. It does. I did get shot. I fully accepted my situation about the same time the surgeons removed the bullet from my back. I was glad to finally have it out of my system—in more ways than one.

Literally and figuratively—and energetically—I got the lead out and moved on. But that little bullet deserved its place on a ribbon alongside my gold and bronze medals. That lead trophy took me places that I never would have gone otherwise. Torrey, sadly, didn't get it out of his system. When his family moved away, he got into trouble a lot—eventually landing in Fort Leavenworth Federal Penitentiary.

Though the bullet was finally out, I still had things I had to deal with (I still do). I had moments of discouragement and despair.

One afternoon my buddies and I went to a sophomore basketball game where my brother Scott was playing—without me. My friends carried me up into the bleachers and set me down on the top row. As the game unfolded, I could hardly watch. I quietly wept, feeling sorry for myself and despairing over the fact that I would never again play basketball with my brother. It was one of my darkest hours—a deep, dark place for me that no one knows about (except you and about 20,000 other readers).

In the years since I was paralyzed, my life has become a demonstration of the power God gives to each one of us to make a personal triumph of our lives. The energy in the promise I made to Him when I prayed for my life after I was shot, allowed me to become a two-time gold medal winner and the only wheelchair basketball player to compete and earn medals in four consecutive Paralympic Summer Games (Seoul, Barcelona, Atlanta and Sydney). I have been honored in my home state of Utah as one of its Top 50 Athletes of the Twentieth Century, and I've served on the Board of Trustees for the 2002 Olympic Games in Salt Lake City.

In 2008 our team—the Utah Wheelin' Jazz—made it to the "Final Four"—the National Wheelchair Basketball Association (NWBA) playoffs. We lost in the semifinals to the Dallas Wheelchair Mavericks who proceeded to win the National Championship. Still, it was a wonderful event. We got to play with the best players in the country. The Wheelin' Jazz has been competing since 1990 and this was the first time we made it to the "Final Four."

In addition, I was inducted into the Wheelchair Basketball Hall of Fame at the awards banquet. This is a wonderful honor, especially for a boy who sat in the shadows in the nosebleed section of the high school gymnasium and wept because he thought he would never play again.

It is also wonderful because I didn't do it alone. My team was right there with me as I received this award. Not just my *basketball* team, but my family and my friends who have been on my team since "shot happened" in 1977.

If you are ever in Springfield, Massachusetts, visiting the Basketball Hall of Fame, do me a favor and go to the wheelchair basketball section and make sure they actually hung my name on the wall.

Dreams and passions don't die simply because we are injured, physically or emotionally. I decided to pursue life with the same enthusiasm I had prior to my accident. I had to focus on what I had left, rather than on what I had lost. I could not allow myself to use my wheelchair as a crutch.

I have challenges, but so does everyone. Except for the fact that I once barbecued my feet, and lost my shorts in a unique manner, I was no different than anyone else.

We all have challenges, whether they're obvious like my paralysis or more hidden, such as dealing with the emotional trauma of a death or divorce. Noted psychologist Dr. Page Bailey said that injury is an interruption of expectations. By that definition, everyone experiences injury. It is then up to that person to create new expectations, and to not allow misfortune to derail their dreams.

My expectations had been interrupted, but I soon learned to expect as much from myself following the accident as I had before the incident—maybe more. I don't like to use the term "handicapped" or "disabled" to describe myself or others (you try playing basketball against the "handicapped" basketball team—you won't stand a chance!) My editor says no one should "dis'" anyone's abilities. I agree with him. I don't want anyone to dis' their own abilities either. Why do we need to say someone is "disabled" or "differently-abled" or even "'specially-abled?" Why do we have to label them at all? We all have special abilities. The greatest disability is to not recognize abilities—especially in ourselves.

CHAPTER 12

One More Dance

Part of my response to life included dealing with my maturing feelings for the opposite sex. With my physical challenges and my reduction in height (from five foot, ten inches standing to four foot, three inches sitting), one might suggest that I wasn't the greatest catch in our high school. But somehow I didn't know that.

I began to date—a lot. It must have been my powerful, electrifying handshake with my calloused, rubber-burned hands that made me especially attractive. I also did wheelies in my chair, which certainly made me the catch of the day.

The fact is, I didn't meet any girls who made it a practice to follow vans with handicapped license plates home in order to date wheelchair-bound guys. But how I saw myself was much more important to my social acceptance than how others saw me; how I saw myself affected how they would see me—and treat me.

This realization wasn't automatic; it came with experience.

I was hesitant to ask a girl to dance. Why would you ask a girl to dance when you can't dance? You wouldn't. You would sit there at a dance, in a corner, feeling stupid, awkward and uncomfortable until some sweet thing took pity on you and asked you to dance—at least that's what I did.

I didn't really want to go to the big dance at Orem High School. But I was home—just sitting there—and that's not where I wanted to be on a Friday night. So I decided to go to the dance anyway. Maybe I'd run into some of my buddies.

The guys were glad to see me—for one second. Then they were off like any other normal teenagers looking for girls. I soon found myself in a dark corner of the gymnasium, leaning back against the cold brick wall. I remember reaching behind me, noticing the slick paint on cinder block and wondering to myself, *Why do they paint brick? To keep it from rusting?*

Then I noticed—or sensed—someone approaching me. I quickly looked down, taking great interest in my shoes. I could see out of the corner of my eye a pair of attractive legs walking purposely towards me. I looked away, then back—and up—and there stood Wendy Castle.

Oh boy, what do I do now?

"Mike, I want to dance."

"Go for it" I thought, "I'd love to watch!"

"Mike, I want to dance with you. Okay?"

I looked up and I was a goner. There was nothing I could do except dance with her or run over her. So I mumbled something unintelligible and wheeled out onto the floor, looking for enough space in which to dance. I was feeling stupid, awkward and uncomfortable. *"This isn't very much fun. Why did my friend shoot me? I'm having a bad day."*

Well, the music was energetic, so I popped a wheelie and started spinning in circles. I twisted and turned to the rhythm of the music and anxiously waited for the song to end. It finally did.

I thanked Wendy for the dance and turned to head back to my safe corner when she caught me completely off-guard with six words I will never forget: "Mike, I want one more dance."

I guess I can do this, I thought. "Okay, sure," I said.

Then the music started and my heart stopped. It was a slow dance. I was stuck and I knew it. Waiting to see what her next move would be, I just sat there—as if I had a choice. Wendy was nervous. I didn't know what to do, and I was sweating bullets (pun intended).

Neither of us knew what to do. She came closer and found herself looking down at me. That wasn't working, so she knelt next to my chair (I was already praying). Other couples danced around us, wondering what we were going to do. Now the pressure was really on. I began patting Wendy on the top of her head to the beat of the music.

That felt pretty stupid. "This isn't working very well and I'm messing up your hair." Then I got a brilliant idea. "Wendy, why don't you sit on my lap?"

She plopped down sideways on my lap and wrapped her arms around me. Momma didn't raise no fool. Suddenly I was no longer embarrassed. I was floating on clouds and discovering a great advantage to being in a wheelchair.

Soon I was back in my corner, leaning against the wall—only this time with a cocky grin on my face.

This was a lot of fun. I was having a good day—and I was the envy of all of my friends.

I had learned first-hand that Woody Allen is right: "Eighty percent of success is just showing up."

I was grateful and happy that I showed up. But I was even more grateful and happy that a wise, considerate, sixteen-year-old girl named Wendy, understood what really makes this world go 'round. It isn't chocolates or flowers or prom dates or movies or new dresses and new shoes, or fancy tuxedos—it is caring and compassion. Wendy could have danced with Roger or Phil or Lance; but she took a chance to dance with me.

And Roger and Phil and Lance were jealous.

What was my *mood* at the dance? Initially, I felt apprehensive and self-conscious. I was feeling sorry for myself. I was scared, nervous and shy. I was wishing things were how they used to be.

My mental *position*, however, was positive. Maybe a better word than "positive" would be *constructive* or *progressive* or maybe *daring*. You decide. I was present and hopeful. My *physical* position was also positive. I had popped a wheelie and was leaning back against the wall. I was present—cool and studly—watching and waiting to see what might come next.

Though I was a bit apprehensive, I operated from the position that everything would work out okay. It did. It worked out better than okay.

We are conditioned to be judgmental, focusing on non-relevant issues, creating stereotypes that limit our vision about people and ourselves. I've found that the happiest, most enjoyable people to be around—and the most effective leaders and managers—are those who look for the good in others. It doesn't mean they are blind to whatever "deficiencies" or challenges they might have; but taking the position to focus on possibilities and not problems is what drives the success of relationships, be they personal or professional.

Thanks to Wendy, I now loved going to dances. My friends started fighting over my spare wheelchair—you can guess why.

CHAPTER 13

Busted

Halloween rolled around and I went cruising with my buddies in Doug Jensen's beat up old sedan. We were out seeing what evil deeds we could accomplish.

I was in the back seat with one of my buddies chucking tomatoes and water balloons at the trick-or-treaters. This was a lot of fun. We had left my wheelchair at home because there wasn't room in the trunk—which was filled with bushel-baskets of soft, overripe tomatoes and a five gallon paint bucket packed with tight round water balloons.

The local police caught on to our pranks, and four patrol cars, with flashing red and blue lights, pulled us over. An officer brusquely ordered us out of the car. My buddies quickly responded. I could only sit there.

"Get out of the car!"

"I can't. I'm in a wheelchair."

"What wheelchair?"

"Uh… I left it at home."

"Sure you did. And tonight's not Halloween, and you weren't throwing rotten tomatoes at kids either! Don't be a smart mouth. Get out, now!" he ordered.

Thinking I was being a stubborn smart-aleck, the officer grabbed me by the shirt and jerked me out of the car. I fell hard against the pavement.

One of the other officers came around to that side of the car. Seeing me on the ground, he quickly explained that I was the boy who had been shot by Officer Fetheroff's son.

Shocked into the reality of my disability—and the unique circumstances of my injury—the officer helped me back into the car. That's an experience *they'll* never forget.

I won't either because I still had to do several hours of community service. I was just as accountable as anyone else. I had always wanted to be treated like everyone else—and I got my wish. I was sentenced to do community service just like my buddies. Of course they gave me a cushy job: I spoke at a local elementary school assembly. That helped start my speaking career—another advantage to being in a wheelchair. Talk about "lemons to lemonade!"

CHAPTER 14

The Flip Side of Giving

Following my accident, I had a hard time accepting help. I just wanted to do it myself. Besides, while in rehab, I had been thoroughly conditioned to the idea that I needed to be independent. I could dress, eat, do chores—whatever—just like anyone, with the help of no one.

I soon learned, however, the position that I need no one's help—I can do everything myself—wasn't the best for me to take. When I allow people to help me, especially when I let them do what they do best, it lets me do what I do best—and the entire team benefits.

Colonel Sanders' business partner, Pete Harmon, who helped him start the Kentucky Fried Chicken chain (just a few miles from where I live) said, "Everyone does something [dang] good. Our job is to find out what it is and let him [or her] do it."

Even in a wheelchair, I can still mow a lawn or weed a garden—and sometimes I do—but why? It takes me a hundred times longer, unless I'm on my riding lawn mower. Except for the time it ran out of gas and left me stranded 100 feet from my wheelchair like it did last summer. It didn't help matters much that no one was home—and my cell phone was in the pouch on my wheelchair.

Don't effective organizations let each team member do what they do best and let others do the rest? That is a win-win for everyone. That is how games—and a greater market share—are won.

They say it's much better to give than to receive; but is it really better, or is it just easier on our egos? As a young man, it was difficult for me to watch my friends help someone load a moving van, repair a roof or build a fence. I wanted to help too. But I slowly learned that sometimes the greatest act of giving is to give someone a chance to help you.

The most effective leaders know that they cannot do everything by themselves or even for themselves. Even if they could, there are others who can do many things much better than they can.

As I wrote this chapter, I heard a speech by Mark Eaton, the legendary Utah Jazz basketball player, during which he recounted advice he had received from the great Wilt Chamberlain. He told Mark to focus on his job. Mark's "job" was not to try to outrun the much faster opposing guards, but to do what he did best: be a seven foot, four inch 300 lb. human wall. His job was to protect the basket, grab rebounds and set up the next play—and let his smaller, faster teammates help him by doing what they do best: carrying out the play and scoring the next basket.

One of the few numbers retired by the Utah Jazz is Mark's #53. He was a below average passer and dribbler—but a phenomenal shot blocker and rebounder—*who knew how to do what he did best.* Following the advice of his mentor, Wilt Chamberlain, he let his teammates help him become an NBA All-Star.

The following saying has guided me for years: "If your lot in life feels empty, build a service station." That's true, but how can I expect others to receive my services if I am too proud to accept theirs? Another trite but true saying is, "When in doubt help people out."

But how *do* you help a stranger in a wheelchair? Just ask, "Can I help?" Let them accept or not as they will. Do they have to be in a wheelchair in order for you to offer your assistance? Maybe a teammate is struggling with a project. Just ask if you can help and let them accept or not.

The idea of letting others help me did not come easy. Gradually, however, I became aware of how important gracious receiving is, both to the giver, as well as the receiver. It helps everyone.

One morning, I decided to cook oatmeal cereal for breakfast. I had the pan on the stove and was pouring the flakes into the boiling water. That round red and blue Quaker oatmeal container slipped from my hands and dumped half its contents onto my lap. I was all spiffed-up in a navy blue pinstriped suit, ready for a successful day—and suddenly

I was covered in dusty pressed oatmeal. I sat there staring at the white powdery mess all over my dark blue slacks while the bemused Quaker gentleman sat there grinning at me from the box.

I rolled out the front door and down to the curb to brush the flakes off my lap into the gutter. I lowered my front wheels off the curb to let flakes slide off my lap.

Suddenly I lost my balance. I toppled out of the chair and into the gutter. My wheelchair tipped over—nearly on top of me. There I sat, with white oatmeal flakes all around me. I looked terrible and felt worse. My next thought was, *Well, I'll just pull myself upright, straighten my chair, and then climb back into it. If I hurry fast enough, no one will notice.*

But someone did. A shiny black Pontiac Trans Am rounded the corner and headed up the street toward me. A wheel was still spinning as if I had crashed at the Indy 500. I tried to look casual, reclining nonchalantly in the gutter beside my tipped over wheelchair. This ploy didn't work, of course. The car pulled beside me and stopped.

The tinted window on the passenger side rolled down and a beautiful young lady asked, "Sir, may we help you?"

"No, thanks," I quipped, "I'm just having breakfast."

Not knowing what to do about this smart-aleck lying in the gutter, the girl rolled up her window and the car sped away.

How do you talk to and treat a person who appears to be struggling with a disability? Like you would treat anyone who appears to be in a difficult situation. Just ask if they need help. If they want your assistance, they will let you know. When in doubt, help people out. Courtesy is always appropriate.

As I struggled back into my chair and then into the house, I felt badly. I had really blown it. I had not allowed others the opportunity to serve me when they wanted to. The worse part of it was that they might never again offer their assistance to a person in a wheelchair—especially if he is in a gutter sitting on his breakfast.

CHAPTER 15

Water Balloons and Rotten Tomatoes

It was another Halloween night full of promise and prospects six years after I was arrested for chucking water balloons and rotten tomatoes. Just before dark, my friend Doug Jensen and I set out to trick or treat at the girls' dorms at Brigham Young University. We were both going to school, and having the time of our lives dating and socializing. On this particular night, as we were going from dorm to dorm, we knocked on the door of destiny.

There stood a strikingly attractive co-ed. We introduced ourselves and Sue invited us in. The boy she was dating had stood her up, so she was home with her roommates, answering the door for guys like us who knew where the action really was.

Sue thought my wheelchair was part of my Halloween costume. Before long, the girls were feeding us Captain Crunch cereal and green grapes and we were laughing and having a great time. Her roommates were surprised that Sue was paying so much attention to me, especially since she had a serious boyfriend. It didn't seem to bother her, though, and it sure didn't bother me!

After a while, Doug decided it was time to leave, so we resumed our trick or treating. The following morning, Sue was talking with the other girls in the dorm about "the guy in the wheelchair."

I really wanted to go out with her but held back for a couple of weeks. I think I was afraid of seeming too eager. Besides, I didn't have her phone number and, whereas "shot happens," I didn't want to get shot down again. Besides, she had a boyfriend who was quite a bit taller than I.

Fate intervened. I ran into her—almost literally—as she was coming out of the university library. I got up the nerve to ask for her phone number and she actually gave it to me.

Our first date was to a pre-season BYU basketball exhibition game, about twenty-five miles up the canyon in nearby Heber City. Since I was the team manager, I knew it would be a good way to impress her. I was driving a late model, white 1980 two-door Pontiac J-2000. I opened her door for her. Then, after climbing into the driver's side, I collapsed my wheelchair and threw it into the seat behind me. I felt pretty manly doing this. Sue was impressed—at least she pretended to be.

We talked nonstop all the way up the canyon. Because I drove my car with hand controls, I couldn't hold her hand. Most girls parents probably wish all college boys' cars—or the boys themselves—had hand controls. I felt really cool and romantic driving my date in my shiny, nearly-new car.

That feeling soon changed. By the time the game started, I got really sick. I don't know what caused it, but I could hardly hold my head up. Sue didn't seem to think less of me, though, and somehow I made it back to her dorm and dropped her off. I was sure she wasn't impressed.

I was wrong. Not long afterward, she agreed to go with me to a campus play, "Singing Sergeants." My family met us there, so I introduced them all to Sue.

By Christmas the flame of love was burning. Sue went home to Ohio to be with her parents for the holidays. She told them all about me.

They weren't happy that she was getting involved with a boy in a wheelchair.

When the holidays were over, I met Sue at the airport. I was dressed to the hilt, decked out in a tuxedo. I took her to a romantic candlelight dinner. The sparks went flying—in both directions!

We dated steadily through the winter semester, and had the time of our lives. She was a beautiful lady with a wonderful personality. Author Michael Nolan said, "Many things catch your eye, but only a few catch your heart. Pursue those!"

And "pur-Sue" I did!

During the week of final exams, Sue began to consider where she would be living in the fall. She had to put down a security deposit to hold a room, so she asked my advice.

I was delighted to advise her to consider Wymount Terrace, a married student housing complex.

She got the hint. Soon we were planning how to deal with her skeptical family. We decided I should fly to her home to get acquainted and get the mystery of the boy in the wheelchair out in the open. She called her mother and told her how serious we were and that she was bringing me home to "meet the family."

After getting the news that I was coming to meet the family, her mother cried for three days. She just couldn't accept the fact that her daughter might marry a paraplegic. She was understandably afraid of the unknown, afraid for what her daughter might be getting into, afraid that she would have to do everything, and afraid that Sue would never give her grandchildren.

I really didn't see myself as being different than anyone else because I wasn't. I just *did* things differently. That's all.

I did understand how they felt, but I knew that in time I could break down the personal barriers caused by their perception of my disabilities.

Things in Cleveland, Ohio, were not easy, though. Once out of my comfort zone, I had a difficult time of it physically. I didn't have my car with hand controls. Their home didn't have a wheelchair ramp. Their bathroom wasn't wheelchair accessible. I had to crawl upstairs, drag myself into bathrooms. Suddenly going from relative self-sufficiency to nearly complete dependence on others for even the simplest things, was humiliating and emotionally disorienting.

Sue came to the rescue. She saw me struggling to crawl up their stairway. She put my arms around her neck and gave me a piggyback ride to the top of the stairs. I was a bit embarrassed and also worried about hurting her—but did enjoy the ride. Her mother raised her eyebrows, but I was in heaven—I could hear the song that played when Wendy once asked me to slow dance—"Stairway to Heaven."

Understandably, Sue's mother and father found our relationship difficult to cope with; however, I didn't let it stop me. My position was that although Sue's parents may feel a little uncomfortable, our life was going to move forward.

Sunday afternoon rolled around and I rolled into the living room and officially asked Sue to marry me. I wanted to do wheelies when she accepted—I was engaged to a beautiful lady! Life could not have been better. I understood her parent's concerns but I had every confidence that they would come around the more they got to know me. And they did.

We've often laughed that we met on Halloween, became engaged on Easter, and got married on our anniversary. But then again, everyone gets married on their anniversary—duh! Although I had to convince my "future-in-laws" that I could take care of their daughter, it was a time of great fun for both of us. Being with Sue was intoxicating. There was nothing I wouldn't have done for her. She made me feel like a million bucks.

We were married August 25, 1984. Sue's family and 1,000 guests attended our reception in the Provo Excelsior Hotel and before we knew it, we were on a delightful honeymoon in San Diego.

We went to the San Diego Zoo and Disneyland, enjoying the balmy tropical beauty of Southern California. It was a time we cherished. We explored our emotions and perspectives, and grew deeper in love. I could hardly believe my good fortune. I was sure she was the most perfect lady in the world.

More importantly, she seemed to love me unconditionally. Your ability to love unconditionally is really tested when your husband is half man, half bicycle.

Sue's family grew to respect and love me. They found out there was nothing I wouldn't do for any of them—not just their daughter.

Two people coming together have enough issues and scripts to deal with without fashioning a marriage around a disability; but Sue accepted me lock, stock and wheelchair.

"Marrying someone who is permanently disabled is a huge risk," she said. "But marrying *anyone* is a risk because we don't really know anyone well enough to make such a commitment—but we do. And this is how it was with us. I wanted children more than anything in the world and I wanted a husband who could direct the course of our family with consistent, gentle leadership."

She knew it was a risk but simply took the *position* that it would all work out.

One of the issues we had to deal with was the expression of intimacy in our marriage. While this subject is sacred and personal, I want to respond to the often-asked, and more often not-asked, questions my audiences have in their minds about it. True intimacy is emotional and spiritual. The physical expression is but a vehicle, a facilitator. We learned together how to be truly intimate. Our scripts and expectations were sculpted by love and admiration and sensitivity to each other's needs. After all, from our perspective this was what marriage was all about.

We wanted a family. We wanted girls as beautiful as Sue and boys as handsome as—well, we wanted boys, too. With the miracle of medical science, we were blessed with three wonderful children. Matthew, Megan and McKenzie. We love them fiercely. What's more, our children even love us—even as teenagers! That's the real miracle.

I remember the night Sue told me she was expecting our first baby. She was excited to share the news with me, and all I could say was, "Wow! That's scary!" (How romantic!) I was overwhelmed with the realization of the responsibility of becoming a father. Matthew was finally born, and while we were concerned about the unknown challenges ahead, we couldn't have been more thrilled.

Soon we added a daughter to our growing family. Megan joined our family on February 8, 1991. I loved being a dad. Our kids never thought of me as a "disabled dad." They did eventually figure out that not all dads are part bicycle, but that never seemed to matter. Their dad may have done things differently, but he did everything other fathers and their children do—and more. We went fishing, played basketball, and I even helped my little Megan decorate her dollhouse. Don't tell me I'm not in touch with my feminine side.

My son was my pride and joy. My daughter was my angel. I was ful-filled as a husband and a father. Life could not have been sweeter. But, I began having the feeling that our family wasn't complete; that we were supposed to have another baby. Sue felt the same way.

We told our doctor of our decision to try for one more child. We needed a fertility specialist. They are expensive. It costs a lot—finan-cially and emotionally—for a paraplegic or quadriplegic to establish his posterity. It had taken many tries to have our first two children, but we had unlimited faith to balance our limited funds, so we pressed forward.

Two weeks passed, and sure enough, Sue was, indeed, expecting our third child. We were ecstatic! Nine months later, McKenzie came screaming and yelling into the world all blue and pink—and beautiful.

She was another miracle baby—another gift from heaven—and like the others, I could not have her near me enough. I was the epitome of "Mr. Mom" except, as I said before, I don't do dishes! I always seemed to know when McKenzie was uncomfortable—as I had with our other babies. Sue once said of me, "One of Mike's greatest gifts is his ability to pick up on the pain of our children—not pick up *after* our children. He has an emotional antenna and quickly detects when one of them is experiencing pain. I think the fact that he is in constant pain, makes him more empathetic than most. The kids love him for it, because he is always able to help them deal with the physical pain and the emotional hurt when they have an illness or injury or loss."

Our children have had tubes in their ears and other common prob-lems. Except for these relatively normal occurrences, we were a healthy, action-packed family. Our biggest problem as a young family was my having to be gone so often because of my Olympic sports activities and speaking schedule.

CHAPTER 16

The Gold Standard

At the ripe old age of twenty five, I played basketball even more than I did as a boy. I had become pretty good at it. I could dribble behind my wheelchair and shoot three pointers. Try taking a twenty-foot shot at a ten-foot hoop sitting down!

Wayne Gretzky, the greatest hockey player ever, said, "We miss 100% of the shots we don't take." Maybe his position about taking risks—taking shots—is why he is a champion. If "shot doesn't happen," you can't score, right? I guess "shot" isn't always bad.

I became a "shooting point guard," developing and relying on my upper-body strength to get the ball through the hoop. Other than the fact that we have to shoot from the sitting position and that we have rubber treads instead of rubber soles, the game is the same. We dribble the ball. We have jump balls—except we can't jump. The same rules regarding fouls and so forth apply. The intensity and skills required of wheelchair basketball players is also the same.

In 1988, ten years following the shooting, another "shot" happened. This time it was a good shot. I had a "shot" at the Olympics.

It was another life changing event. I was asked to try out for the U.S. Paralympic basketball team. I was pursuing my MBA at Arizona State University in Tempe, and the tryouts were being held in nearby Tucson. The top sixty wheelchair basketball players in the United States were invited.

I gave it my best shot and made the team. I was the youngest player to be selected, and was ecstatic at having the chance to wear the red, white, and blue jersey in the Seoul, South Korea Paralympics.

The Paralympics is the second largest sporting event in the world—a sister organization to the Olympics—consisting of athletes with physical disabilities. They are held in conjunction with the Olympics, one week later, and always in the same city. Thousands of spectators are inspired by the grit and determination of these excellent athletes as they watch the competition from opening to closing ceremonies.

Years ago, Paralympic athletes were a curiosity, written up in the life style pages with the focus on our disabilities and the "human interest" of overcoming personal disaster. That has its merits, I suppose. But now the news focuses—as it should—on the athlete and the game. The Paralympics are now considered a "serious" athletic event and that makes sense to me.

Wheelchair athletes are not the only ones who compete in the Paralympic Games. There are athletes who deal with blindness, spina bifida, dwarfism, amputation and other physical limitations. I shouldn't say physical "limitations;" I should say physical "variety" because, believe me, these athletes are anything but limited.

As the United States team was boarding the planes bound for Korea, I found myself surrounded by 400 athletes, trained to be the best.

It took four hours to load the athletes and their equipment onto the airplanes. The wheelchair athletes were the first to board. They stowed our chairs and the flight attendants asked us to remain seated while the others boarded (as if we had a choice).

We arrived in Korea and were bussed to the Olympic Village, accompanied by an armed escort. I could hardly wait for the games to begin. Before I knew it, we were in the gold medal game, playing against the highly touted Netherlands. Although I was the only rookie on the team, I was privileged to be the starting point guard.

During the half-time chalk talk, it really hit home to me the quality of the event I was participating in—and the excellence of the athletes involved. This wasn't a second rate display of talent, but a game involving the finest athletes in the world. What's more, they were athletes who, in every case, had overcome tremendous personal difficulties before joining the team.

I began to realize that they weren't great in spite of their obstacles in life; they were great *because* of their challenges, or rather, because of the momentum acquired as they rose above their challenges.

As a youth, I dreamed of being a professional basketball player. I was five foot, eleven inches. The odds were steeply against my ever succeeding at pro ball. But now, at four foot, three inches (sitting down), I was playing for the greatest athletic trophy in the world—an Olympic gold medal—and I was confident we would win.

And win we did. The score? Fifty-five to forty-three! I was delighted to have scored eight points, but ecstatic at how well we played as a team. Each of us did our job. We mastered the teamwork attitude essential to success in any organization. Selfishness and grandstanding were eliminated. We each played our role and achieved together the highest level of success possible in the world games.

Twenty minutes after our victory, we rolled out to listen to the national anthem and watched as they raised the flag of our great country to the rafters in the center position. As we were presented our individual gold medals, I felt those powerful emotions experienced by athletes who win the gold. My eyes blurred with tears as I remembered only ten years earlier lying in a hospital bed, wondering if I would ever play basketball again.

When I got home, Mom was so excited about my gold medal, she wanted to bronze it!

One of the first friends I made after arriving at the Olympic Village was a French athlete. He was a mighty four foot, two inches—standing up. I loved hanging out with him because he had a great sense of humor—and he made me feel tall! He was an eighty-pound weightlifter who bench-pressed somewhere around three hundred pounds. He said he could do it because he didn't have to lift it as high as anyone else. He only had to push it fourteen inches! But I don't think I could bench press three hundred pounds even one inch.

I have seen a man with one leg jump over a seven-foot high bar and another long jump twenty-two feet. I saw a one-armed man with no legs swim—*fast!* I have seen blind runners outdistance their competition and sat fascinated watching a team of blind athletes play a game called "goal ball" (similar to soccer). The ball is electronically programmed to "beep" repeatedly so that the team members could locate it.

I realized that these are real athletes who can out run, out jump, out shoot, out maneuver and out persevere almost any mere mortal. Olympic-level success always depends on Olympic-level positioning. What is "Olympic-level positioning?" No matter the difficulty, the pain, the challenge, the disability or handicap—or the mood one might be in—it is overcome by adopting the position that we keep moving (limping, tapping, or rolling) forward.

And what if we are in a bad mood and need to cheer up? Look out, hotel staff! You might become victim to one of our pranks. One day we stuffed our little weightlifter into a pillowcase in our room in the Olympic Village and hid around the corner waiting for the maid to show up. As she stripped the beds and shook out the pillows, she was shocked to see a little human tumble out of the pillowcase. We didn't exactly understand the language she spoke, but we did get her meaning!

It was a lot funnier to us than it was to her.

My best memories were not just about winning the gold, but of the entire journey to the Paralympics and the athletes who inspired me. It was an intense and action-packed experience—one I'll always remember.

Four years after competing in Seoul, I found myself again on an airplane traveling with my teammates to Barcelona, Spain. As I trained hard to make the team, my motto was "No pain—*no Spain!*" This would be a journey of destiny, only not the kind of destiny we anticipated.

Nice pants! It's 1976.
I'm with Great Grandpa
Warner and my brother
Scott who is holding my
little brother Todd.

Nice wheels!
Getting used to my
new life shortly after
my accident.

Fishing a few years before my accident. I've always loved the great outdoors.

Still love to fish—even from a sitting position.

Finishing my
first marathon
in 1981—on
a flat right
tire (fishing is
easier)!

My amazing parents and six siblings. They've always been there for me.

Tami's and my engagement photo. I am a lucky guy.

She loves me. It's written in stone (okay, just sand; but still good).

September 2, 2000. Tami took a seat on my lap. I didn't mind!

Coach is behind me yelling "Don't shoot!" but I shot anyway. Proof that "Shot Happens"—even in basketball.

Climbing a hill in Southern Utah. Life Rocks! Keep pushing forward.

Everybody has to have a "bucket list."

Even more excited about getting bounced by my wife and kids on the trampoline. A strange sensation when you can't feel your legs or butt.

2000 Olympics in
Sydney, Australia.
We didn't lose the Gold;
we won the Bronze.

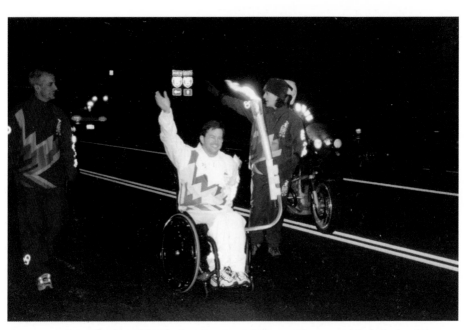

Carrying the Olympic Torch for the 2002 Winter Games in Salt Lake City.
Smiling but nervous I might drop it. Thanks, Mom, for nominating me.

Jumping snowmobiles with my son Matt and basketball teammate Rodney.

Broke my ankle in 16 places on this very jump. I'm still limping a bit.

Celebrating our World Championship with Trooper Johnson
and Reggie Colton.

A stop at the White House to meet the President on our way to the
1998 Olympic Games in Altanta, Georgia.

Nice set of wheels. I mean the titanium wheelchair.

Tide is coming in. Up to my neck in problems at the beach in San Diego.

Cruising the neighborhood in a hand cycle.

"Hey kid! Better get your foot out of the way. I'm not stopping."

The family all decked out in camouflage. Can you find all seven of us?

Okay, a bit easier to see what we look like. We have kids in college, high school, middle school, and elementary school.

Hang on! Don't let go or things will get worse.

Sometimes I get tired of taking the elevator (there never seems to be anybody behind me).

Two gold and two bronze medals and an Olympic Torch. I have become a collector of "heavy metals." I feel blessed to have represented our country for almost 20 years.

I actually work once in a while. Mowing the lawn and painting the ceiling.
I swallowed a lot of paint. I prefer mowing, unless I run out of gas.

Reuniting with Torrey —a special moment for both of us.

Sharing my life's experiences at a corporate event in Minnesota. I enjoy inspiring, motivating, and entertaining others.

CHAPTER 17

Everything You Do Affects
Everyone on Your Team

The 1992 Summer Olympics and Paralympics to be held in Barcelona were anticipated by the media to be the best ever.

They certainly were for us. Once again we were presented gold medals while the national anthem played and our flag was raised to the center position. Once again we had gone the distance, beating the Netherlands by three points. Once again we were the best in the world. Once again my mom wanted to bronze my gold medal.

But she didn't have the chance, because I lost it.

A certified letter arrived one morning stating that our entire team had to return our gold medals, or we would be barred from Olympic competition for life.

The Paralympic officials had randomly selected one of our star players for a drug test—and he tested positive.

The night before the gold medal game, he had awakened with severe phantom pain, common to paralytics. Without thinking, he took a prescription painkiller. Perhaps because it was three o'clock in the morning, he failed to follow protocol. Perhaps he didn't think about the fact he was in violation of the rules intended to prevent the use of performance enhancing drugs.

Sending our medals back, after having worked our hearts out to win them, was one of the most difficult things any of us ever had to do. In fact, one of my teammates refused to send his back. It was the only gold medal he had ever won. He was never allowed to play again.

I don't harbor ill feelings toward my teammate whose actions caused us to lose our gold medals; still, it is important to remember that one errant action by one member of the team cancelled several thousand hours of work and sacrifice by the entire team to achieve a team goal. The error of one hurt us all.

Though this was frustrating and discouraging, I have since used it to remind myself, my clients and audiences that everything you do affects everyone on your team.

In the past, I have told this story without revealing my teammate's name, but now I will tell you who he is. He is Dave Kiley—one of the greatest wheelchair basketball players ever. Although he was banned for a time from the games, he continued to serve the association. He was, in fact, eventually elected Commissioner of the National Wheelchair Basketball Association (NWBA).

Though his mistake cost me a gold medal, Dave became one of my best friends. He recently spoke at my induction into the Wheelchair Basketball Hall of Fame.

His positive positioning, relative to some very tough circumstances, demonstrated the magnificence and leadership of this great athlete.

CHAPTER 18

Chuckin' Wheelchairs

The games were held in Atlanta, Georgia, in 1996. Because of my previous two competitions, I was now a veteran. I was going to have fun winning another gold medal to replace the one taken away from us. That was my position—I would have sweet revenge.

The Paralympic experience was tremendously valuable to me. Rubbing shoulders with the great athletes of the world gave me wonderful perspective and insight. In addition, although Sue had attended the first two Paralympics with me, this time we would be taking our ten-year-old son, Matthew. This would be a very special family outing—my son would watch his dad win the Olympic gold. At least that is what I thought. What I didn't know was that I was about to be taught a lesson worth more than a gold medal.

As expected, the red, white and blue progressed undefeated to the semifinals. Then we faced off with Australia. We were favored to win. After beating Australia, we would play Great Britain for the gold the following evening.

We did well, leading through most of the game; however, one of Australia's players, Troy Sachs, was hot. He played the strongest game of his career, scoring forty-two points. We lost at the buzzer by a single point. It was humiliating for us to lose our first Olympic game in ten years in front of 10,000 spectators in our own country. Everyone, especially us, knew we should have beaten them. We didn't know how to handle it.

Coach Hedrick came into the locker room and started chucking wheelchairs. Some of us were still in those chairs! We simply did not know how to lose. Well, obviously we had just learned how to lose; we just didn't know how to *handle* losing! Eventually Coach refocused on the task at hand and gave us an encouraging speech that settled us down and emotionally prepared us for our final game.

We played Spain the next day for the bronze medal and won by a healthy margin. We played hard, but it seemed strange to fight for third place. We were spoiled and a little elitist, weren't we! The one consolation in winning the bronze instead of the silver is that silver medalists *lose* their last game!

Since receiving this bronze medal, I've had fun showing it to audiences. I especially enjoy pointing out the Braille inscription on the back for the blind athletes. While rubbing this inscription, I tell people that it says, "Australia kicked your butt!"

I went home and threw this important Olympic medal unceremoniously into a sock drawer. My attitude really "socked" didn't it! I was being Crappy Schlappi again. We had gone from winners to whiners.

As I thought about it, I realized that if I felt humiliated with an Olympic bronze—if I felt embarrassed by being a member of one of the top three teams in the world, instead of number one—then I needed to start thinking differently. Third place in a world of seven billion people wasn't so bad. I must be a pretty good athlete and I should focus on that.

I, therefore, re-evaluated my position and took a more constructive stance. We would get back the gold in Australia in 2000! At the ripe old age of thirty three, I may have been pretty far along to be an Olympic athlete; but because the Aussies had beaten us in Atlanta, I was determined to get back at them by beating them on their home court.

Little did I know, however, that things were about to change on my home court.

CHAPTER 19

Broken

Going through a divorce was something I never once thought would happen to me and my family.

In 1999, Sue informed me that she wanted to end our fifteen-year marriage. I was stunned—and then deeply depressed. This was more paralyzing than the impact of a .38 slug from a police special. I made mistakes that caused some of the breakdown of our marriage, but I had worked my tail off for a different conclusion than what eventually took place.

Ultimately, my wife's decision became final, legal and permanent. After meeting with our three children, I became resigned to having a broken family.

Was my family really broken? It was changed. It would function, but differently, even as I had learned to function differently. I was determined that my family would continue to be successful and happy. That was my position. Still is. We had a great family. Still do.

I assured our kids that Mom and Dad both still loved them dearly and, even though we would be living in different households, we would continue to have the same "Mom and Dad relationship" with them.

I began to be a father from a distance—but not too far. Sue soon remarried. It would have been so much easier for me to move away—and get away from the pain, but I chose to stay in the neighborhood. I had chosen to maintain my relationship with my kids and I stuck to that position.

"Shot Happens" and it happens more often than most of us would like to acknowledge. There are so many paralyzing events that occur, but I have long believed that when difficult things happen, the Lord in His tender mercy brings a compensating blessing. In my case, this blessing came in a package of three and arrived in my darkest hour.

One day, as the ripples of divorce gradually subsided, my sister Collette mentioned that there was someone she wanted me to meet—one of her closest friends—Tami Gibbons—a newly widowed mother of two. Tami had been happily married to her husband, Rich, and together they had brought Joseph, Robbie, and Anna into the world. Robbie, however, had been born with a congenital heart defect. After several open-heart surgeries and many traumatic days dealing with his pain, he passed away. He was barely two years old.

Just before Robbie passed away, Tami's husband was diagnosed with an inoperable brain tumor. They tried every form of alternative medicine to arrest the tumor and prolong Rich's life; but their efforts were futile. He died in April, fifteen months after the loss of their son.

Tami was nine months pregnant with their baby at the time of her husband's funeral. The day after he was buried, Tami went into labor and gave birth to their third child, a beautiful girl she named Anna Richey.

The next year was extremely difficult for Tami and her two living children, but she was determined to make the best of a terribly difficult situation. Tami truly believed that "things turn out best for the people who make the best of the way things turn out." That was her position—and still is.

Tami and I met on March 28, 1999 at a church choir concert. Tami was the conductor. There *was* electricity. Afterward, Tami walked into the foyer. I was there with my three children and my parents. Everyone conveniently left the building, so I could become acquainted with the lady I had been dying to meet.

My son, Matt, had gone home with my folks, taking the key to my van. What a tragedy—or was it "strategy?" Seeing that I was stranded, Tami offered me a ride home. I transferred to the passenger seat and waited as she wrestled my wheelchair into the back of her van. I felt helpless, and self-conscious; but Tami was a caregiver of the first order. She handled the situation so casually that I didn't feel embarrassed.

Tami was stunningly beautiful, intellectual and engaging. We laughed and joked as if we'd known each other forever. Our personalities meshed and within two months we were engaged. We were prayerful about this decision and felt sure of ourselves.

What we didn't anticipate was the roller coaster ride our relationship would experience over the next eighteen months—because of me. I wasn't ready to get married again. The pain of divorce was still deep and I needed time. Although we were "on and off again," we always came back to each other. I needed to date others, which I did, but every time Tami came out the winner. Actually, I was the winner because Tami is a jewel. Her love and loyalty to me were more than I deserved.

> *"The last straw," Tami remembers, "was the annual July 4th Stadium of Fire celebration at Brigham Young University. I went with a date and we took my son Joseph and two of his cousins.*
>
> *"As we were walking around the stadium, looking for something to eat, we saw Mike from a distance. It had been six weeks since we had broken up and I was not prepared for what happened next. Suddenly I had a difficult time breathing. Joseph saw him in the same instant, ran up and threw his arms around his neck. Mike was buying pizza for his friends and seemed really happy to see us.*
>
> *"It was very awkward for my date, who was ordering pizza, but I had to give Mike a quick hug, too. We chatted for a minute, at which time my date walked over to ask me what kind of pizza I wanted.*
>
> *"Mike tried to stay cool but those dark eyebrows of his raised about six inches. I loved it. Well, what did he expect? Did he think that he was the only one who could date others? (Ha!)*
>
> *"We went back into the stadium—me with my date and Mike with his buddies—to watch the show; however, I don't think either Mike or I enjoyed the fireworks. I couldn't stop shaking for what seemed like forever."*

I was surprised to see Tami. I was across the stadium from her and kept my binoculars trained on her most of the night. She was even more beautiful than I remembered and I realized how much I missed her. I didn't know how serious she was about the "pizza guy," so I figured I'd better find out—now.

I had recently purchased a home in Draper, Utah, to be near my children. My friend, Nick Hess, was living in my basement apartment, so I drove home to drop him off. Then, with Tami's address flashing on my emotional GPS, I spun the van around and drove all the way back to Pleasant Grove.

I pulled up in front of Tami's house and called her on my cell-phone. It was one o'clock in the morning, but I needed to talk to her and see where we stood—where *I* stood.

Tami answered the phone. When I told her I was parked outside, she laughed and invited me in. We talked, and I told her how long the past six weeks had been for me. She had experienced the same feelings. Before long, we were in each other's arms. Our emotions were strong and beautiful and the weeks apart melted in minutes.

After a long talk—and longer kisses—I finally went home. I was re-committed to our relationship. She was too. Having both been married before, we visited a counselor about how we could deepen our relationship and move forward.

Reflecting back, Tami says, "Some of my family and friends were apprehensive that I was marrying a man with a disability. But Mike's chair was never an issue. I loved Mike for the incredible man he was, a consistent model of perseverance, determination and a positive attitude (I suppose I should now say "positive position"). I was not just attracted to him (you must admit, though, he's cute!), I was in love with who he is."

I invited Tami and her kids to come to the Schlappi Family Reunion. There they could get to know Mammy and Pappy Schlappi and the Happy Schlappi clan. It was being held at the Camelot Campgrounds near Strawberry Reservoir in the beautiful Uintah Mountains in northern Utah. The date was July 28, 2000. This was not going to be an ordinary family picnic. Tami tells it like this:

> *Everyone but me was gathered at the fishing pond at the other end of the campground. The "fishing pond" was that familiar*

game where a child throws a line over a barricade, then waits for a fish to "bite." When there is a tug, the child pulls it back and finds a prize clipped onto the end of the line.

I was still back at the motor home at the campground when Mike's sister-in-law, Becky, came to find me. She insisted that I hurry down to the fishing pond game immediately.

I didn't think anything of her request—until everyone prodded me to fish. When I finally said I would, I noticed Mike's brother-in-law Troy, hiding behind a tree with a camera. My heart started to pound as I contemplated what might be on the end of my line. Long seconds passed; then there was a tug. When I pulled my line back, I saw I had caught a little green velvet box!

I began to cry. My kids didn't have a clue as to what I was crying about. I opened the box and saw a ring that was so much more than I felt I deserved, and so beautiful.

I had known Mike's family for over a year and I loved every one of them. I wanted to be a member of that family so much and it felt great to officially become part of it!

Yes, Tami was excited; but no more than I was. My heart was beating a hundred miles an hour as I slipped the ring on her finger. It fit perfectly and the real celebration started.

Within sixty days, Tami and I were married. We went to Lake Tahoe for our honeymoon and it was wonderful. We were truly in love. Remember what I said earlier about compensating blessings? The Lord had answered our prayers and though we would go through difficult times (and great times) blending our families, traditions and customs, I knew we would build a solid marriage. I felt the healing begin—for both of us.

"I had been through a great deal," Tami said, "but I believed in prayer. Mike and his children were an answer to prayer—our blended family is full of love and our children get along wonderfully. Marriage hasn't been without its difficult moments, that's for sure, but after all we have been through, our lives are again filled with happiness."

Often people are curious about the intimate details of our marriage. Can we be intimate, physically? Are our children ours? We explain that we are very happy with our marriage and with each other and, yes, they are our kids—all of them.

We have fun. We swim, camp, and fish together. We love going to our family cabin in the mountains. Despite my being in a wheelchair, we do everything a family can do together. We snowmobile in the winter and ride four-wheelers in the summer. I am a mobility equal! Then we play card games and board games and drink hot chocolate until everyone falls asleep.

We love our family traditions. One of these is our annual Christmas Eve excursion to see the lights. We vote on the homes best decorated and come up with a winner. We sit around the kitchen table, light candles, and each of us expresses what we are most grateful for. I am always most grateful for them.

If you ask my kids what their favorite family memories are, they will tell you how much they really love our annual family vacations. I use my frequent flyer miles and take the whole kit' n' caboodle on family vacations. We have gone to New York, Orlando, Wisconsin Dells, Hawaii, and Washington, DC. Once I took my daughter Megan to Cancun with me on a speaking assignment.

Our children still enjoy looking over my calendar and choosing one or two places they'd like to visit with me when I speak. We've had a lot of fun over the years and enjoy some wonderful memories.

One of the most enjoyable things I do with my kids is wrestle with them. They love ganging up on me, pinning me to the ground by sitting on my paralyzed legs. When they feel they have tortured me enough they let me up—but not until I promise to take them for ice cream.

When they were really little tykes, we'd play "the foot game." I'd get out of my wheelchair and lay on the floor. They'd take off a hundred miles an hour (or so they thought) and try to get past me before I could grab their feet. They would wiggle and giggle and laugh 'til they were out of breath. And it was—and is—wonderful.

CHAPTER 20

Faster, Higher, Stronger

The most powerful chess piece is the Queen. The King is the most *important* piece—capturing the King ends the game; but the queen is more versatile. She defends the King. Without the Queen, the King is toast.

Not long after Tami and I were married, my goal of participating in a fourth Paralympics became a reality. I was delighted to be selected to represent the U.S.A. in Sydney for the 2000 Paralympics. I would be one of only two or three wheelchair basketball players to have competed in four Paralympics.

I left early for Sydney, Australia, and trained with my team in order to become acclimated to the time change. Being away from Tami was tough. We spoke regularly on the phone, but that wasn't enough. I wanted her to be *with* me. We had been married five whole weeks and it was clearly time for a second honeymoon!

"Being away from Mike was hard," Tami said. "I needed to be with our children, but I had heard so much about the Paralympics and really wanted to personally witness every minute of this amazing event that had been so much a part of Mike's life.

"Mike knew that I wanted to experience the entire event so as a birthday present (for me? or for him!) he flew me to Australia early so I could enjoy the opening ceremony as well as every game on the schedule. This was the best birthday present I could have asked for (that and the fact that he actually remembered my birthday!)."

Tami finally arrived (along with my parents and other family members) for the games. Having them all with me meant everything. They stayed in a motel, while I stayed in the Olympic Village with my team. It was definitely not the way I wanted our second honeymoon to be. Of course, I admit I smuggled Tami into the Olympic Village on a few occasions. I'm sure she didn't look suspicious with all five foot, seven inches of her crouched behind my chair. Sometimes she would just walk in masquerading as an Amazon athlete.

> *"When I arrived at the opening ceremony," Tami recalled, "I was so excited I could hardly stand it. I hadn't seen Mike yet, and with more than 120,000 spectators and athletes milling about, I wondered if I would be able to find him—so that I could get my ticket!*
>
> *"The U.S.A. athletes were some of the last ones to enter the stadium. The basketball players were lined up outside the arena in their red, white and blue star-studded wheelchairs ready to roll into the stadium for the opening ceremony.*
>
> *"I was so excited when I saw my new husband that I ran and jumped onto his lap in front of everyone. We were kissing and hugging and I was in seventh heaven being there with Mike! I didn't want to let go, but after a few seconds, I heard the U.S.A. team chanting, 'Tami, Tami, Tami...' so I blushed, jumped off his lap, grabbed my ticket and hurried to my seat so I could take pictures of him and the team as they rolled into the arena like conquering gladiators."*

Seeing Tami was the shot I needed. We'd only been apart for ten days, but it seemed like an eternity. Having Tami at the games made a huge difference for me. Even if we couldn't be together much of the time, I know I was "faster, higher, stronger" because she was there. Cervantes was right, "Woman is the soul of man; the radiance that lights his way."

As we prepared to play our first game against the team from South Africa, I had time to think about what led up to this day and the little bit of history I was making. I was the first wheelchair basketball player ever to participate in four consecutive Paralympics. I could hardly wait for the games to begin.

Training had been difficult over the past four years as I dealt with the disruption of heartache and divorce and slowly regained control of my life—as much control as you can have when you are married with kids. But that was now behind me and, as I said, life was good.

I actually began playing competitive sports in the community Bantam League when I was eight years old. I played baseball, basketball, and football and loved them all. What made things even more fun, as I got into basketball, was that my dad was always my coach. He was a real people builder, and instilled in me the belief that I could do anything regardless of the circumstances.

I wasn't just a pampered kid who spent his summers attending one basketball camp after another. Instead, my dad ingrained within my mind the need to practice hard all the time so that I could always be on my game, even when things were difficult.

I remember winter mornings, getting up when it was still dark, shoveling snow off the driveway, and then shooting baskets for an hour prior to heading off to school. That position of preparedness paid off.

Mom was always at my games, cheering me on. Both parents had their own way of motivating me and I would never have made it to the Olympics without them. I was so glad Mom and Dad were there to witness this incredible event. My mother is writing her memoirs. One of her chapter titles is "Once a Cheerleader, Always a Cheerleader." She had been a cheerleader in high school and now she was an "Olympic cheerleader."

A word about competition. I believe my success in athletics has a lot to do with my position with regards to competition. How do I compete with my opponents? I don't. I compete with myself. Beating others in order to prove that I am better than they are feels rather shallow. Challenging *myself*, however, to reach my highest possible level regardless of what others are doing, is more important. Challenging ourselves to go "faster, higher, stronger" is what matters most.

The Paralympic Games of 2000 soon began and we found ourselves facing the South African team. I was the starting point guard and couldn't have been more psyched when the whistle blew to signal the jump ball. Dave Kiley, my former teammate whose positive blood test had cost us the gold medal in Spain, was again on the team. He had paid his dues to redeem himself and now we were going to have some serious fun.

Our team won the first game and my stats were good: twelve points, seven rebounds, six assists, and three steals. Unfortunately, as the games progressed, I spent fewer and fewer minutes on the court. The younger players gained confidence and experience as we advanced all the way to the medal rounds. Not playing as much as I was used to was hard for me, but I took the position that it was good for them rather than bad for me—that it was good for the team and therefore good for me—and that is what counted. When I wasn't playing, I would sit back and take in the experience. It couldn't have been more rewarding.

We finally got to the semi-finals playing against the highly-rated team from Holland. Things didn't go our way, however, and by halftime we were down by fourteen points. In the closing minutes of the second half, we narrowed their lead to two points. My teammate fired off a three-point shot at the buzzer, but it wasn't meant to be. We found ourselves once again playing for a bronze medal.

We were devastated, just as we were in the previous Paralympics. Twelve big muscular guys were crying like big babies—right along with the coach. It was especially hard since we had won the World Championship two years earlier. Seeded Number One, we had been the favorites going into the games—and now we had to fight for *third place!* It's like kissing your sister.

The next day we were scheduled to play Great Britain for the bronze medal. Déjà vu? We had done this before, hadn't we? Not really. This was a different team and we had a different attitude (and I had grown up a lot in the past four years). Sure, we were deeply disappointed, but this time we mentally prepared for the game by focusing on what we had to gain, not what we had lost.

There were 20,000 fans in the stands, everyone was screaming for their favorite team and players. Earlier in the tournament, we had beaten Great Britain in overtime, so we knew we were in for a dogfight.

I had become a collector of "heavy metal" and I wanted to return home as a four-time Paralympic medalist. I had already won two gold medals and one bronze. I wanted to balance out the set.

As the game progressed, it became more intense. It was indeed a dogfight. Now there were five seconds to go and the score was tied. Great Britain had the ball. The crowd was out of control. My heart was in my throat. All my energy was focused on winning.

One of Great Britain's players drove in for a lay-up. He missed. We grabbed the rebound.

Barreling down the court with the ball, one of our young players, Paul Schulte, flew over the half court line at full speed and launched a thirty-five foot shot. It is an impossible shot, especially for someone in a wheelchair. (He was sitting down, for Pete's sake!) There was no jump or spring from healthy legs and feet. Except for the forward momentum from his chair, he had nothing to propel the ball that kind of distance but arm and shoulder muscles wearied from a high intensity, high energy, high-level game.

The roaring crowd fell breathlessly silent as the ball arched through the air and "swooshed" through the hoop touching nothing but the bottom of the net just as the buzzer goes off!

Pandemonium erupted as we piled into a scrambled mound of wheelchairs and players. Somehow I found myself on the bottom of the pile—upside down, like a stranded turtle, but I didn't care. I was part of the wonderful Olympic experience—and won a bronze medal—and completed my set!

The place went nuts. I was amazed to be so happy—a very different emotion than the depression we felt when we had received the bronze four years earlier. What was the difference? We still had the same result—the bronze medal. But this time our position had shifted. We hadn't *lost* the gold—we had *won* the bronze.

We were in the top three of all the teams in the world. Not bad! Besides, my mom wouldn't have to bronze this one either.

Soon after, we were received our medals—and I was silently thanking my Creator for giving me such a rich experience—and for adjusting my attitude so I could truly appreciate what was happening. "Shot happened" and it was "a shot *seen* round the world."

Faster, higher, stronger? You bet! Flying home (in the plane) at 33,000 feet, I had a chance to sit back and analyze my life. It had taken unexpected turns, to be sure. The "shot" that happened when I was 14 was life altering, but I had a beautiful wife and five incredible kids who called me, "Dad." My faith in God, and myself, had grown ever stronger. I had now earned four Paralympic medals representing the United States in the greatest sporting event in the world—and none of it would have happened if "shot" hadn't happened.

CHAPTER 21

Dorf on Golf

When we resist change, we fail. When we accept change, we survive. When we create change, we succeed.

Anonymous

What is the most important change we can create? A change in ourselves. In our attitude. Our perspective. A change in our *position*. The way we look at things—think about things and, ultimately, the way we do things.

When we think about things differently than we might have at first—when we take a different position—we achieve a result that is much different than the circumstances may at first dictate. A change in our attitude, our perspective, our *position* towards our circumstances—creates opportunity where once was challenge, and success where once was failure.

Why do we meet at conventions? Well, to convene—to meet—and enhance each other through our association with each other. I am a keynote speaker. I am paid well for what I do. Why? Because, like Domino's, I deliver. What do I deliver? I deliver a difference. What kind of difference? Different results—improved productivity, enhanced profits, etc.

Now, how does one lone fellow in a wheelchair create such a difference? By affecting a change in the people who deliver results—affecting their position towards themselves, their companies, and their world.

When I help people positively and constructively shift their positions with regards to their work, their coworkers, their company—even the economy—their behaviors shift and positive results follow as naturally as a wheelchair rolling downhill.

The most important asset in any organization of value is its people. Not money, not equipment, and not real estate. Do you want to affect results? Then affect your people—positively.

> *"…Your most valuable resource is your human resource! Money and property just sit there in a pile until a human being does something with them. Humans operate and maintain your equipment, real estate and buildings. Humans manage your money. Humans solve your problems and discover or create opportunities. Humans create, produce, market, and sell your products or services. Your human resource manages all your other resources so you can prosper…"*
> —Tom Cantrell, *"are you a C.E.O. or a P.O.W."*™

To move to a higher level of corporate effectiveness, then, you *must* move to a higher level in how you deal with your number one asset: people. This book is about simple solutions. How's this for simple—simply shift your position towards your people—including yourself (always remember, "your people" includes you!) and watch your assets increase.

> *"…It takes greater patience, insight and ingenuity to manage human resources than any other resource. Neither money nor property care how they are used. Humans do. Trucks don't care if other trucks get better paint jobs. Computers don't care if they are used to play solitaire or balance the budget. People, however, have values (not always noble values!) and complex (and sometimes rebellious) minds. They care what they do, why and how they do it, and how they are treated or regarded in the process."*
> *[People] must, therefore, be managed with inspiration and respect for individual values, talents, personality—even idiosyncrasies—even disabilities.*
> —Tom Cantrell, *"are you a C.E.O. or a P.O.W."*™

In the foreword of this book, I suggested that every one of us suffers some kind of disability—physical, mental or emotional. But are we *disabled*? No. No one is disabled—unless they are dead. Think about it. A computer that is "disabled" is unplugged. A bomb that is disabled is rendered completely ineffectual. An engine that is disabled is dead stopped. A computer or engine may be limping along with reduced capacity but as long as it works to some extent, it is not technically disabled.

So it is with us. We may be limping (or rolling) along, but we are not disabled. As long as we live and breathe, and function with purpose, we can affect change. We may suffer handicapping conditions that may range from mild to severe, but nothing that I know of, except death, disables us.

At the risk of raising the hackles of the "politically correct," I prefer to accept the athletic term "handicap"—as in golf. Remember what Mr. Dorf (Tim Conway) said about the game? "Why do they call it 'golf?' Because it is the only darn four letter word they had left!" When you have a golf handicap, it simply means you need a little accommodation to bring you to a level playing field with the other golfers. That's all.

But I digress. This isn't about disability awareness. This is about *ability* awareness and recognizing how much each individual contributes to organizational objectives when we shift our position toward our circumstances and begin to genuinely regard challenges as opportunities.

So, recognize that tough conditions or situations are no more or less disabling than the position we take towards them.

As an expert witness, I can get on the stand and make the point of why life in a wheelchair is a handicapping condition (bladder and bowel problems, social stigma, constant physical pain and discomfort, constant inconvenience, and reduced physical ability or dexterity). I can also testify why it *is not* disabling (I am a successful athlete, parent, speaker, author, etc.). In no case, however, can I in good faith testify that anyone is one hundred percent disabled—unless they're dead—much to the chagrin of certain attorneys who would like their clients to be awarded a million bucks per limp.

Disabled, differently abled, handicapped, physically challenged, mentally challenged, dominant hand challenged (left-handed)—how about "Dysconvenienced?" Whatever you call it, it isn't my job to define or label the difficulty. It is my job to suggest an appropriate response and position relative to your difficulty—whatever encumbering situation it is that you may be encountering. I'll leave the labels up to others.

Why don't we just consider differences as just, well, *differences*? Why label them at all? Some suggest that maybe we just consider them human imperfections or inconveniences or limitations that everyone has. That is fair, but I don't even see them that way. Differences are not limitations. They may be inconveniences, I'll agree to that, but they are not necessarily limiting. These "dysconveniences" can, in fact, become advantages if you know how to use them.

My editor is an amateur magician—a pretty good one, if you ask him. He is also visually impaired (which might explain some of the "creatively spelled" words in this book—"dispelled" words, he calls them). He gets around via public transportation. He says, "I can drive but the pedestrians don't like it." He suggests that his magic is better *because* of his disability, not in spite of it. His "visual dysconvenience," helps him "see" better what the audience "sees" when he disguises his movements so they can't see it at all.

I don't get it. I thought his magic was real.

I have a friend who has obsessive compulsive disorder (OCD). Several of his family members have it as well. His aunt has it. His mother and his sister also suffer from the same disorder. It may be inherited. What is their compulsion? Everything has to be even and balanced. If he scratched one side of his face he had to scratch the other side the exact same way with the opposite hand. If he stepped on a rug with one foot and not the other he had to go back and step on it with the other foot.

It is a terribly frustrating and, depending on its severity, it is a sometimes debilitating disorder. Have you seen the television series "Monk?" That is a dramatization of obsessive compulsive disorder. My friend doesn't "suffer" from it now, however—it now serves him. He overcame the need to act on it years ago, but because he had it so severely when he was a youngster, he learned to use both hands to do most everything equally and evenly.

He is now essentially ambidextrous. He works his computer mouse with his left hand and the number keys with his right and handles the computer much quicker and more efficiently than he ever would have had he not had the disorder—the dysconvenience—when he was younger. He also uses the creative right and the logical left side of his brain more equally and is one of the most brilliant creative professionals I have known. However, without his having had the "dysconvenience" of being obsessive-compulsive in the way he was when he was a youth, he wouldn't have developed the level of talent and productivity he has today.

My friend, Brad Barton is dyslexic. His little "b" and little "d" look the same to him, so he sometimes spells his name "Brab," so we call him "Brab." He is also an author and a speaker and a professional magician. When you ride with him, though, don't tell him to turn right, he will turn left or drive straight through the intersection while trying to figure out which is right and which is left.

He always felt like he was imperfect and lacking, because of his "dysconvenience," but then he came across a book called *The Gift of Dyslexia*. It explains that dyslexia is not necessarily a disability; it is often evidence of a high level of creativity, etc. The book listed dozens of incredibly talented and creative individuals with this dysconvenience and suggested their talent was a result of, or linked to, the dyslexia and they were successful *because* of, not in spite of, the dysconvenience.

Who were these dyslexics? Hans Christian Andersen, Bruce Jenner, Alexander Graham Bell, George Burns, Cher, Winston Churchill, Leonardo da Vinci, Walt Disney, Albert Einstein, General George Patton, William Lear, Charles Schwab, Woodrow Wilson and Jay Leno—and *Brab* Barton.

In his book *Beyond Illusions*, Barton says that *The Gift of Dyslexia* helped him come to more fully appreciate "the gift this supposed disability really is." In this insightful book, Ronald D. Davis writes:

> "*Dyslexia is the result of a perceptual talent, an asset which in some situations becomes a liability.' He reveals that this multi-dimensional visually fixated perception style creates the vulnerabil-*

ity for confusing symbolic information processing. Davis added, 'It can also make people imaginative, inventive, able to think on their feet and react quickly. They are often good athletes, conversationalists and good story tellers.' "

In *Beyond Illusions*, Brad continues, *"Imagine my relief to learn that Hans Christian Andersen, Bruce Jenner, Alexander Graham Bell... etc... are all dyslexic—just like me! Where once I saw liability, I now see opportunity because I elevated my thinking. I look with a different set of expectations and create a better paradigm."*

What gives me the right to address the issue of dealing with and appreciating "dysconveniences" with such authority? Well, just being paralyzed doesn't make me an authority on disability issues any more than living in a garage would make me a car. I'm not a disability expert—I am an attitude expert. It was my mental and emotional position relative to my circumstances that created my success and made me an "expert" in my area.

What was my area of expertise? Helping individuals adjust their position relative to their circumstances. I served eight years with Intermountain Health Care as a Director in the administration of their rehabilitation programs. For several years my title was Director of Attitude Therapy. My job was to help individuals with newly acquired disabilities (I mean *dysconveniences*) believe that there was life and hope despite their injuries—just as my "roll model" Mike Johnson helped me believe.

I've always been reluctant to expose my weaknesses, especially after my accident. I'm sure that going from a popular young athlete with no real problems—and a lot of real success very early in life—to suddenly being slammed to the mat by a misguided bullet made me more sensitive to this than I may have been otherwise.

I have always been driven to succeed. Perhaps this deep yearning to succeed at the highest possible levels is a compensation for the paralysis I deal with. I may be limited to what I can accomplish physically; however, I have never felt limited, overall. I may be limited in what I can *do* but I am not limited as to what I can *accomplish*. I've earned an MBA, served a mission for my church, won four Olympic medals, and have been inducted into the Hall of Fame. I have enjoyed a dream career of being a professional speaker and have authored this book. Most importantly, I enjoy life with a wonderful family.

I do not mean to sound boastful; I could have accomplished nothing without the inspiration and support of my family, my friends, and my God.

Dad gave me my will to win and showed me that I could still be a great athlete. Torrey taught me the power of forgiveness—especially self-forgiveness—and to move forward (and not play with guns). My siblings gave me the confidence needed to know that I could move forward.

My first dance partner, Wendy, showed me that I was still loveable and worth someone's time and attention. My beautiful wife inspires me to stay focused on my vision and purpose. My children motivate me to keep doing what I do and Grandma Schlappi taught me to laugh through the pain.

The list goes on. My friends, my professional speaker colleagues, my coaches and teachers, my creative editor and my mom who, within days of the shooting told me, "If you can't stand up, you can still stand out."

Shortly after my accident, I realized that I needed an outlet for my changing but still valid athletic ambitions. I decided to start "running" marathons. (A marathon is twenty six and two-tenths miles.) I loved the challenge, but more important was what I learned in the process.

I bought a used racing wheelchair (with the cool rakish wheels that keep you from flipping over on a fast turn) and, in the early spring of 1981, began to train in earnest. On July 24 at six o'clock in the morning, the race began—for the wheelchair athletes. We started about ten or fifteen minutes before the "able-bodies" so they didn't get their shoelaces tangled in our spokes when they took off (I refer to them as the "ABs").

The first thirteen miles was uphill. Can you imagine? Pushing your wheelchair up the steep incline of the Wasatch Front—in the Rocky Mountain range? What a way to start my day! In three miles my shoulders began to ache, in five miles my hands began to get sore—but the real problem began over my left ear and progressed through my brain to the other side of my head.

I began to doubt. I began to be discouraged. I began to despair. What am I trying to prove? Who cares if I do this? What's the point?

The folks who started me off with cheering and encouraging applause had faded into the distance. All that accompanied me was—me. Even the other wheelchair athletes had spread out over several hundred yards and I was essentially alone. A dark "FUD" cloud—Fear, Uncertainty, and Doubt—formed over my head like the dark thundercloud that always hovered over the unfortunate little Joe Btsflk in the *Lil' Abner* comics of the sixties.

Most of the ABs had passed me. One runner in a bright yellow jersey, trying to be encouraging, patted me on the shoulder as he passed, saying, "Good job. Don't quit. You're an inspiration…"

Thanks, I thought. *Shut up. Wait 'til the downhill…*

Seven miles. Blisters began to form on my hands. I was staring down at the brownish-blue mountain asphalt with sweat running into my eyes and dripping off my nose.

This isn't very much fun. Why did my friend shoot me? I'm having a bad day.

Then I realized that staring at the ground was not only boring, it was pulling me as far down as I was looking. Without thinking about it, I suddenly did the one thing that has helped me as much as anything else in my life.

I looked up.

Suddenly I saw trees and blue sky and white clouds and a beautiful winding road that led up and up—to my goal. Energy flowed through me and my chair almost leaped forward as if pulled by an invisible rope. Where did this energy come from? The same place it always comes from. Within. Remember, all motivation is self-motivation. The goal is the motive. Get to the top of the hill. Why? Because it is all downhill from there.

The ABs were far ahead of us. They had in fact pretty much forgotten us. There they were jogging happily down the other side of the mountain when a sinister sound imposed itself on their peaceful descent. It started as a whisper—a subtle whine of rubber wheels on asphalt. Can you imagine looking over your shoulder and seeing eight broad-shouldered deep-chested athletes in wheelchairs bearing down on you at forty miles an hour? Talk about chariots of fire!

I passed the guy in the yellow jersey. As I spun past him, I patted him on the butt and said, "Good job. Don't quit. You're an inspiration. See you at the finish line."

As I wheeled towards the finish line, hundreds of spectators came into view, clapping and cheering. Through my sweaty grin, I wondered, *Three hours ago you were at the starting line and now here you are at the finish. That's great, really it is, but where were you while I was on the mountain?*

I realized that a marathon is much like life. At the beginning, people cheer us on and encourage our efforts. Likewise, they are there to cheer us across the finish line. But what about the really tough part? The three hours in the middle? The twenty-six miles in between the start and the finish? That is where we are alone. That is where we are weighed and measured.

It is in those times, when no one is watching, that integrity and character are determined. It is also in that place of solitude that our true attitude—our position towards the things that happen to us—is identified to oneself, the one who really matters in the race. It was there that I discovered all motivation is self-motivation (there is a lot of time to think about things while pushing a wheelchair for twenty six and two-tenths miles!)

Although support from others is important, in the final analysis, it is our mental, emotional and spiritual position—and the decisions we make based on our position—that determine our results.

CHAPTER 22

The Rest of the Torrey

Audiences often focus on my injury, as if paralysis is the only difficulty I have to contend with. They are often surprised when I tell them that, just like themselves, I deal with all types of difficulties. ("Dysconveniences," remember?) Life is full of dysconveniences—for everyone, not just someone who lives in a wheelchair. Everyone has headaches and heartaches. They are simply more obvious or dramatic for some. Depression can set in when a business deal goes sour. Anger and frustration arise when faced with doubt, debt, d'inlaws—d'IRS!

It is true that for every one of us "shot happens!" Credit is shot? Marriage shot? Career shot? Attitude shot? Well, *shot happens!* Disability, depression, discouragement, debt, death, divorce, doubt—*dysconveniences* happen.

In fact, the emotional and spiritual dysconveniences we experience usually far exceed any physical problems we might have. In fact, the extra weight of these unresolved issues we carry around with us robs us of energy and encumbers our journey through life.

By the way, what happened to Torrey? Maybe I should say whatever *became* of Torrey—we already know what *happened* to him—he accidentally shot his best friend and shot happened to him, too. He went through shock, denial, guilt, and remorse—what we don't know is how he ultimately responded to what happened to him. In my first book, I told how after the shooting, he moved away, eventually married and had a son—but then tried to live life by his own rules. He did hard time at Fort Leavenworth Prison, and lost everything.

At least that is what I reported in my first book. Would you like to hear, as Paul Harvey refers to it, "The rest of the story"?

It has been my goal—my prayer—that Torrey and I could meet again, so for the past few years I have tried to find him, or at least find out about him; but he seemed to have virtually disappeared (a lot can happen in thirty years). I finally located Torrey's family. They told me he was out of prison and back in Utah. I gave them my phone number and asked if they would have him call me.

A few days later, I was having lunch with a couple of my wheelchair basketball buddies when my cell phone rang.

The voice was quiet and familiar. "Hi Mike... This is Torrey."

It was as if a bridge suddenly spanned the time and distance. I was surprised and excited, "Torrey! Where are you?"

He was only about three miles away on the freeway. He took the next exit and headed for where I was. I waited anxiously and when he walked in the door, decades disappeared. I am an Olympic athlete and he has been pumping iron in prison for twenty years—hey, we looked *good!* We even have our own hair and teeth!

We stuck out our hands to shake, but hey, this is Torrey—he went down on one knee and enveloped me in a bear hug—and thirty years melted away.

With the noise and my other friends there, we couldn't really talk, so we set a time to meet a couple days later.

It was an amazing meeting. Torrey and I talked, we laughed, we argued about how it all really happened, and (I hate to admit this, and tough ol' Torrey will *never* admit it) we even got tears in our eyes.

As I said, Torrey looks really good. He is in excellent physical shape and he is handling the tough process of gaining acceptance in a sometimes unforgiving society. I am proud of him. He has been out of prison several years, has found a good relationship and is moving up in the construction industry.

Torrey has taken a positive position relative to his circumstances and is responding to life accordingly. None of us understand how tough it is for a convicted felon to believe on the inside that he can make it on the outside. We don't know how tough it is for Torrey, but right now his life is in a much better position than it has been for many years. And now you know "the rest of the Torrey."

I often wonder why we are given the paths we are given. But I have faith that everything happens—even shot happens—for a good reason. Or perhaps we just make a good reason out of what happens. Either way, it works. It's all about *position* after all, isn't it?

About the Editor

Why would I write about my editor? Because he deserves the acknowledgement! Creative Editor of many books for speakers and writers, Tom Cantrell is known for his ability to hear what authors want to say and to say it the way we mean to say it. He shares our vision and takes it—and us—to the next level.

Author and speaker in his own right, his greatest calling, however, is to inspire and empower others to change the world by saying the right thing at the right time to the right people in the right way. His common challenge to us is, "Go deeper."

He is a presenter and clarifier of ideas that challenge the standard of common thought—and he gives those ideas away as fast as they come to him. He helps us get real. In quietly serving us, he epitomizes the words of Albert Pines: "What we have done for ourselves alone dies with us. What we have done for others in the world remains, and is immortal." That is what a Creative Editor does. That is what Tom does.

Thank you Tom.

If you want Tom Cantrell's assistance on a book or project, call me. Or you may contact him directly at:

Tom@TomCantrell.com
TomCantrell.com
801-355-2005

About the Author

Despite apparently limiting circumstances, Mike Schlappi envisioned lofty athletic ambitions and enjoyed wonderful achievements. His objective now is to take his modified—or *clarified*—definition of "attitude" to the world to enhance the way we respond to challenges.

Member of the National Wheelchair Basketball Association Hall of Fame, Olympic Gold Medalist, Certified Speaking Professional, MBA graduate, licensed Financial Advisor, husband, and father or five, Mike has been an international keynote speaker for twenty years.

This entertaining and deeply inspirational speaker considers it an honor to set the tone and reinforce the theme at corporate conventions, and other professional and public events.

Mike's universal message is simple and profound. When "Shot Happens" it can be a great blessing—provided we deal with it from the right position.

Would you like him to speak to your organization? Would you like to order additional books and products? Visit Mike's website or contact him directly.

MikeSchlappi.com
Mike Schlappi Communications
641 East Pheasant Haven Ct.
Draper, Utah 84020
Phone: 801-553-MIKE (6453)
E-mail: Mike@MikeSchlappi.com